5-Year Crusade

The Easy Way to Achieve Your Impossible Goals

John Soforic

5-Year Crusade / John Soforic
979-8-9928960-4-6

Crusade: *a vigorous, life-changing movement to advance a worthy cause.*

Contents

Prologue 1

The Wealthy Felon 3

5-Year Crusade 7

The Power Within 15

Self-Shackles 27

C *is for* Clarity 41

R *is for* Restore 51

U *is for* Unlearn 61

S *is for* Sacrifice 77

A *is for* Activity 89

D *is for* Daily 103

E *is for* Expect 117

S *is for* System 135

Closure 149

5 Years Later 163

Now What? 167

Crusade Resources 173

Self-Shackles Questionnaire 183

The Crusader's Creed 186

Start Here 193

A Word From The Author

After publishing *The Wealthy Gardener*, I contracted COVID-19 and experienced long-term cognitive issues, including brain fog and dementia, which limited my activities to reading an hour a day of Harry Potter. It lasted over a year. During this spell, I stopped practicing the daily habits and routines that had once shaped and defined my life.

As the brain fog lifted, I didn't regain my previous capabilities—I was slower, less sharp. Eventually, I decided to revisit the lessons from a book I had been working on, *5-Year Crusade*. It reminded me of the power of consistent, small extra efforts and habits, repeated day in and day out, that had built my success during my five most productive years.

When I was at my best, I worked a full-time job, built a rental business to over 100 units, managed a house flipping business, finished a triathlon, gave 10 weekly hours to an AAU basketball program, maintained a strong marriage, raised two children, earned financial independence, and paid cash for three college educations. Most importantly I was enthusiastic and excited about life. I followed the crusader's way, day in and day out, as outlined in this book. I felt alive and energized.

But after COVID, I felt like an invalid just trying to learn to walk again. I devoted two years to reworking, rewriting, and revising the daily system of *5-Year Crusade*, even discarding two completed and professionally edited manuscripts. As my cognitive faculties improved, the essentials of this book became clearer. In many respects, *5-Year Crusade* saved me at a time when I needed traction and direction in my own life.

Long story short, I regained my power and completed not only this book, but also the *Daily Crusade*, the *Crusader's Planner*, the *Crusader's Tracker* app, the 5yearcrusade website, and launched a little website called the Wealthy Bookheads.

The point I'm making is that anything and everything is possible within a few short years. All you need to do is to build your inner power and engage it with focused daily effort.

The system of a five-year crusade is outlined in this book. I have written it in fiction format as the sequel to *The Wealthy Gardener*, although it can surely stand on its own. Thank you in advance for giving it your time, attention, and consideration.

I pray that this book helps you as much as it helped me during my recovery. You will be challenged at the end of this book to achieve four winning weeks in a row. By then you'll know what this means, and I promise that it's easier than you think.

The system is the solution. Just try it. Keep score. Track what you do. Control your mind. Expect more. Follow the system. Exercise. Plan your time. Do the little extra efforts day in and day out that lead to meaningful results in the next five years.

Just win today, repeatedly, and you'll be fine.

5-Year Crusade

Prologue

Five years ago Jimmy buried his mentor, the man who was like a father to him. Five years ago, he honored the dying man's final request to continue teaching his weekly class at the juvenile detention center. Five years ago, he taught lessons from a syllabus that was the mentor's legacy of wisdom on prosperity. Jimmy did his duty, taught the classes, and mastered the lessons.

Four years ago Jimmy looked like a winner. He owned a property management business that virtually printed money. People called him a natural, a gifted entrepreneur, a wealthy outlier. He was a former juvenile delinquent who'd achieved financial freedom and had made it look easy.

Three years ago, Jimmy started drifting—sleeping in and skipping morning routines of exercise, goal focus, meditation, and prioritizing days. He started aiming for a more balanced life of part-time work, home chores and an overabundance of leisure. He'd earned the right to relax and, at his level of success, he could easily coast with no immediate consequences.

Two years ago, Jimmy started to lose ambition. He sensed that his fire, discipline, and drive were slipping away. He felt less happy and more unsettled; maybe it was just the effect of being 30 years old. When teaching at the reformatory, he grew frustrated with himself and the students. Was it meaningful to teach a course that didn't seem to change behaviors? Was it hypocritical to advocate principles that he didn't embody himself?

One year ago, Jimmy disappeared. He went on a retreat to a

beach, where he sat in the sun to enjoy the good life. He found days at the beach to be easier with a drink in his hand, and so he parked his chair near a tiki hut bar most days. Jimmy made friends, pursued pleasure, and found misery. With all the freedom in the world, he was lost in days without purpose.

Six months ago, Jimmy left the beach and returned home to create a masterclass designed to help juvenile delinquents. In the process, he rediscovered the essentials of success—daily activities, everyday routines, extra effort, and weekly impact hours behind his financial achievement. Ultimately, this course gave him what he needed most: the missing piece of his lifestyle puzzle. He committed to something he loved—and what he loved was far more than he could have ever imagined. . .

CHAPTER 1

The Wealthy Felon

Don't let your wounds turn you into someone you are not. You're not your mistakes. You have nothing to prove. A bright future awaits you, but only if you forgive yourself for the mistakes of the past.

– Lessons of the Wealthy Gardener

In a sparse conference room at the juvenile detention center, five serious administrators gathered around a sleek, polished table. The room was cold, with bare walls and a small window showing the sky through bars. At eight sharp, the reformatory's Superintendent walked in and quickly took his seat.

"You know why we're here," the man said. "Jimmy's waiting outside, and before we let him in, I wanted to talk privately. He taught a class here for several years, then disappeared for a year. Now he's back with a completely revamped curriculum. Did everyone review the course manual?"

All heads nodded affirmatively. On the table in front of each administrator lay a booklet titled *Behavioral Wealthology: The Study of Wealthy Behaviors*. It was a controversial proposal to

3

consider—a new course aimed at teaching incarcerated youths how to achieve audacious money goals. Although an elective class, it contrasted sharply with mandatory prison courses on anger management, substance abuse, vocational training, and basic life skills aimed at reacclimating the kids into society and preparing them for ordinary paying jobs.

"The course objective," the Superintendent said, "proposes small efforts that in aggregate constitute the 'easy way' to achieve difficult goals. The theme is a 5-year crusade, working steadily for five years to achieve uncommon, life-changing results. Jimmy chose five years because two-thirds of our juvenile delinquents return to prison within five years of discharge. Lastly, he's teaching this class pro bono as 'an experiment' to change that problematic statistic."

The Superintendent eyed the others present at the meeting: the Academic Director, Clinical Director, Case Manager, Oversight Committee Representative, and Educational Program Coordinator. This last person, Sara Ruggeri, 31 years old and three years into the job, was the only female in the room. She was also the person most likely to oppose the unorthodox course.

For fifteen minutes, the group engaged in a collective debate about the proposed curriculum. A sticking point that proved unresolvable was the concept of a *Power Within*. The course was built on a thesis that goal achievement is an inner game of unshackling this inner force—the ideal self, an innate intelligence—whatever you want to call it. The six administrators argued without progress about this abstract concept.

In the end, Sara took control and redirected the discussion despite her junior position among others at the table.

"With due respect to all," she said calmly, "we're mandated to report new programs to local government authorities, child welfare agencies, and the juvenile court systems. What are the instructor's qualifications?"

Jimmy's former case manager took the lead. "He was a juvenile delinquent, but since parole he's become a wealthy young man. Jimmy's a natural winner—one of those rare people who makes entrepreneurship and wealth look easy. He's had a string of business successes, starting as a realtor and ending as the owner of a property management business. He seems to crave goals and at times needs to prove himself—maybe to make amends for his past felony. Lastly, his parents abandoned him in juvenile detention, and he's since refused their attempts to reconcile." The summary ended abruptly, and the room was quiet.

"What was his felony?" Sara asked.

"Involuntary manslaughter," the case manager said. "On his sixteenth birthday, he got drunk, drove his car into an oncoming vehicle, and the other driver died."

Another awkward silence.

"A wealthy felon," chuckled the Oversight Committee Representative. "Well, isn't that rich? We got ourselves a course on making money by a wealthy felon."

The other administrators grinned awkwardly in response, but Sara wasn't amused. While not a fan of the course, she believed in the mission of a juvenile detention center. She'd taken this job to rehabilitate youths and help them. She also passionately believed in the principle of second chances.

"Do you define yourself by past mistakes?" she snapped.

The older man's jaw dropped. "Excuse me?"

"I think her point is that Jimmy's paid his debt to society," said the Superintendent. "He's a wealthy ex-felon who committed a crime when he was sixteen. In the end, maybe that's the best reason he's qualified to teach incarcerated youths how to achieve audacious money goals."

The Superintendent stood. "Let's bring him in."

CHAPTER 2

5-Year Crusade

Five years is the farthest I plan now. It's a long enough stretch of time for our actions to change everything, and it's a short enough span of time to manage. Anything and everything is possible with the steady use of days in a 5-year crusade.

– Lessons of the Wealthy Gardener

Jimmy sat in the open chair at the table. Dressed in tan slacks and a collared shirt, he appeared poised, physically fit, and intense. He greeted each administrator warmly and even said hello to Sara Ruggeri, calling her by name, although they'd never met before today. Scanning the table, he sensed a tone of opposition. It was the *Power Within*, an intangible instinct that spoke without words.

"So here we are," Jimmy said. "I taught a course for years as the surrogate for my mentor, and now I want to teach my own system."

Everyone at the table nodded silently. It seemed they expected him to continue, but Jimmy simply allowed the silence.

"Let's hear more," the Superintendent said. "We were all very comfortable with the course you've been teaching. Why are you changing it?"

Jimmy leaned forward. "I'm not changing it; I'm streamlining it. I want a system of actions, not just principles. Prosperity is a way of life, and I want to teach this way of life. Success is the sum of small efforts day in and day out, and I want to teach these small efforts. I've seen kids try to win goals the hard way, and I want to show them how to win the easy way."

"About that," Sara Ruggeri said tersely. "I'm the Educational Program Coordinator, and it is my job to ensure that elective courses align with the goals of our institution and meet best practices of educational standards."

Jimmy folded his hands on the table.

"I've read through your syllabus," she continued. "Your course is about daily actions and habits—what you refer to as the Crusade Way—to empower marginalized youths to save $100,000 within five years after their discharge. So, my first question is, do you really think that's possible?"

Jimmy didn't flinch. "Yes, it's possible. Not only is it possible, I'll teach them to practice expecting it."

Sara smirked faintly. "Why is money the goal of your course?"

"The ambitious kids are already motivated by money," Jimmy said. "I want to keep it simple—appeal to their existing desires, and then teach a system to achieve impossible goals."

Sara raised an eyebrow. Her first impression of him was quick and harsh. *What an uneducated know-it-all, thinking his success in business makes him an expert in behavioral change and prison reform.* She'd seen this act before—an arrogant fool who can't appreciate the complexity of psychology or social disadvantage.

"Excuse me," she said finally. "Did you say you'll recommend *impossible* goals to the boys?"

"Yes, goals they don't yet know how to achieve," Jimmy

answered, "using powers they don't even know exist."

The other administrators nodded in response, but not Sara, who remained impassive. Looking at her now, Jimmy knew exactly who his opposition would be today. His first impression of her was quick and harsh. *What an overeducated know-it-all, thinking her college degrees made her an expert in real-world success.* He'd seen her type before—an academic idiot who was too educated to appreciate the value of simple, mundane, everyday strategies.

"About the concept of a 5-year crusade," the Superintendent said, steering the conversation to calmer waters. "Can you elaborate on this unique framing?"

"A 5-year crusade is a simple lifestyle," Jimmy said, "made up of mostly good days strung together for a cause. It's just one good day and then another good day. Small efforts lead to good days. And a lot of consistently good days lead to big years and extraordinary goal achievements."

Jimmy offered no more, and the table was silent.

"And it takes small efforts?" Sara said skeptically. "Your course is based on the thesis that success is easy?"

"Yes, success can be easier than you think. And no, not just small efforts, but daily small efforts," Jimmy clarified, sensing the meeting was becoming a one-on-one debate with this attractive but off-putting woman. "It's making small efforts, avoiding small errors, winning one day at a time, and ultimately, being intentional to achieve big goals."

"Be specific," Sara snapped. "What small efforts?"

Jimmy opened the course manual to a specific page. "It's all written here. These eight principles form the basis of the course."

The only sound was the rustle of paper as the others read from their manuals.

C-R-U-S-A-D-E–S

C — **Clarity:** *You are what you do today.* Focus on what you want most, why you want it, and what you'll do to earn it.

R — **Restore:** *Calmness is power.* Dissolve your stress and restore your mind with physical movement.

U — **Unlearn:** *Your vices are just habits that feel good but harm you.* Unlearn your vices with a habit fast.

S — **Sacrifice:** *An extraordinary life requires the sacrifice of ordinary things.* Sacrifice the many ordinary things that matter least to your goals.

A — **Activity:** *Doing the right thing is more important than doing things right.* Prioritize the vital few things that matter most to your goals.

D — **Daily:** *Success is the sum of small efforts repeated day in and day out.* Make small efforts, one day at a time.

E — **Expect:** *You get in life not what you want but what you expect.* Practice expecting more.

S —**System:** *You don't rise to the level of your goal; you fall to the level of your systems.* Follow a tracking system.

"So these are the principles for the course," Jimmy explained. "Each principle will have a weekly lesson plan. Each lesson has homework in the form of small daily efforts. By the end of the course, the students will track their daily performance of these eight principles. They'll use a checklist and a scorecard."

Sara examined the list. She did her best to hide her contempt—not over the list itself, but with the C-R-U-S-A-D-E-S acronym, which reinforced her view that this course was a superficial conglomeration of pop psychology.

"And these eight principles," Sara said in a tone that didn't mask her cynicism, "free an entity you call the *Power Within?*"

"Yes, the system is built on empowering the inner force," Jimmy said flatly, "and then engaging this force."

Sara exhaled audibly. "So if I sat in on the class, what would be my top takeaways?"

Jimmy thought for a moment. "I promise to teach you a prosperous way of life. I promise to show you that it's easier than you think to win audacious goals. I promise a one-month challenge to prove it. And I promise a system of achievement to free your *Power Within* so that you'll experience your full potential."

Sara paused, considering a sharp response.

"*THAT'S a splendid idea!*" the Superintendent boomed.

Sara recoiled. "What's a splendid idea?"

"Your idea to oversee the class," the boss responded.

Jimmy glanced at Sara. He immediately sensed an inner calm, despite the surprise. The meeting ended, and Jimmy alone left the room.

The administration voted to accept the course on a trial basis with supervision. Sara was tasked to meet with the instructor before every class to discuss content. She'd also attend and evaluate classroom presentations, with full authority to pull the plug at any time.

As the group filed out, Sara shook her head and opened the course curriculum to examine it more closely, now that she had been assigned to supervise this weekly class.

"Lesson Plan 1: The Power Within."

Sara closed her eyes and groaned.

Part One
Self-Empowerment

CHAPTER 3

The Power Within

Power Within: *inner wisdom; mental force; spirit*

Your mind is the Unseen Power, the essence of your potential, the core of your being. You control it, or you control nothing. A controlled mind is the force that compels the actions, choices, work, and struggles behind every worthy achievement. You each have a God-like potential in your minds, and you are accountable for it above all else. You honor it, or you waste it.

– Lessons of the Wealthy Gardener

During the week since the meeting, Jimmy managed his property business, acted as trustee for an endowment fund that supported juvenile detention centers, polished lessons for Behavioral Wealthology, and attended college to earn credits for a teaching degree—an interim step on his way toward a doctorate.

He tracked his good habits, bad habits, work hours, and, lastly, the number of free hours devoted to his dreams. He called the extra work in his free time his "impact hours," and this additional effort was the most important factor in a 5-year crusade.

During this particular week, he also investigated the history of the adversarial Sara Ruggeri, the one person who seemed to pose an immediate threat to the course and his long-term vision for it.

Jimmy probed her background with admiration mixed with wariness. Sara had surprisingly come from a wealthy family and had graduated from an Ivy League school. She now held a bachelor's degree in psychology, a master's in education, and a second master's in social work.

Most impressive to him, however, were the hardships she had endured to achieve this education. Sara gave birth at twenty-two, became a single mother, worked a full-time job, and somehow managed to earn her two additional degrees in her free time. She now lived with her daughter's father in an arrangement of convenience.

Professionally, at the juvenile detention center, Sara was known as an idealistic reformer, always trying to revamp the mandatory curriculum but endlessly frustrated by her lack of autonomy. She was unpopular, didn't seem to mind, and regularly challenged the administration. For unknown reasons, Sara stayed in this unsatisfying job despite its challenging aspects.

Jimmy looked at her now as they sat alone in the conference room before the inaugural class.

"I'm honored you volunteered to sit in on the course," he said with a sheepish grin. "I think it's a splendid idea."

"The honor's all mine," Sara replied curtly. "I'm hoping to learn from the best—the top graduate of our detention center."

"Flattered," Jimmy said, playing along. "What would you like to talk about first? I know a lot about everything."

"My first concern, among many," Sara said seriously, "is that this *Power Within* notion might lead these kids astray, chasing ludicrous money goals without being grounded in reality. Why is it even necessary to discuss it in a course on success?"

"It's important to acknowledge our greatness," Jimmy said, "since only with such a belief can we expect great things."

Sara paused and bit her lip. *I knew it. Here we go with the self-help fluff talk.* "Have you considered the harm of excessive self-esteem? Research shows that the model backfired. It seems too much ego can indeed lead to too little effort."

Jimmy nodded. "I'm not advocating too much ego, and in this course, you will not see too little effort. When we think of inner power, I agree it can go off the rails; we can believe in innate potential to the point of narcissistic overreach. I get that completely. But a worse problem is that we can underestimate our full potential, which is an even worse form of self-delusion."

He watched her twirl a pencil in silence.

"What exactly is the *Power Within?*" she asked.

"Some people call it the mind. Some call it the spirit. Some say it's the subconscious, the soul, or even divine intelligence. Maybe they're all describing the same thing. I don't need to know what it is to know it's real. I just know that when I ignore it, I tend to drift. When I align with it, I tend to rise."

"You can't define it?" Sara asked. "I'm supposed to approve an elective course centered around a premise you can't define?"

"I'm not sure I want to define it in exact terms. Call it your inner compass, your untapped mental potential, or your spiritual core. I don't care what name you give it. What's important to know is that it's the part of you that wants to grow."

Sara looked at him for a long moment.

"I don't know what the hell it is—but I know it's in there," he said. "What I know for sure is that we have to cultivate and free this inner force to achieve audacious goals."

"Well, let me play devil's advocate and challenge your theory," she said. "I've earned audacious goals. I've achieved hard things. I never had to cultivate this mystical *Power Within.*"

"Maybe you come from a background that cultivated the *Power Within* for you. Is it possible that you come from a family where success is expected and wealth is normal?"

Sara felt instantly defensive, pausing to stay calm. Was he speaking of her background specifically or figuratively?

Jimmy continued, "If you don't need to do the inner work that is required by some of us for outer success, that's an enviable position. But for me, and most kids in a juvenile detention center, it takes some inner work to overcome our past conditioning. This course is for people who feel trapped in life."

Sara studied him. "Fine, give me an example. How exactly do you cultivate and free this theoretic *Power Within?*"

Jimmy summarized his journey from juvenile delinquent to his current position. The story was one of rising and falling, an endless loop of ups and downs, the direction of which was always determined by small habits and hours that defined a daily lifestyle. He told of his start at a minimum wage job, how he became a realtor, founded a property management business, inherited a trust fund, and achieved his goals of success and wealth. In the end, he took a vacation and came undone in a mid-life crisis that devolved into an emotional and mental meltdown.

Sara studied him curiously. She wasn't expecting a shallow rich guy to admit vulnerability. "You fell apart recently?"

"Yes, not long after I achieved my dreams," he said. "I started drifting, and in the end, I had to rebuild myself again."

"What did this rebuilding look like?"

"It looked like the same old habits and daily disciplines that I'd followed to achieve my initial success. I clawed my way out of the darkness one day at a time. I focused on the person I wanted to become. I cultivated a winning mindset. I faced my inner demons in order to free my best self and engage again."

Sara looked curious. "What demons in particular?"

"Self-imposed demons," Jimmy said.

"Such as?"

He sighed. "I isolated five personal issues. My inner demons consisted of self-delusion, self-neglect, self-sabotage, self-doubt, and self-contempt. I wrote an affirmation statement describing the person I would be without those five inner demons. Then I recorded this statement on my phone and listened to it every morning to set my mindset. It was a practice of self-suggestion—a form of cognitive restructuring—to revive the *Power Within*."

Sara studied him, surprised to hear a behavioral psychology term coming from an uneducated guy. "Let me get this straight," she said pensively. "You made a personal affirmation statement to review daily, describing the qualities and behaviors of the person you'd become without your inner conflicts?"

"Yes, to cultivate the *Power Within*," Jimmy said, "and to stay focused on the simple daily habits most people skip. I did it to train my mind and reset my mental patterns. I called this affirmation statement my 'Crusader's Creed.'"

"That's different," she said. "Did it work for you?"

"Yes, it did—but I didn't just listen to affirmations. I also used a daily checklist to hold myself accountable for intentional behaviors and daily choices. What are you getting at?"

"Share your Crusader's Creed with the class," she suggested. "Show the kids how you 'clawed your way out of the darkness' and restored your inner power. Consider incorporating these affirmations into the course, and don't hide your vulnerability. You did it yourself; why not teach it to the boys?"

Jimmy froze at the suggestion. He felt natural resistance, but something deep within told him she wasn't wrong.

Sara leaned forward. "This is a course on achieving audacious goals, and the *Power Within* is the main thing, right?"

Jimmy sighed, gazing at the small, barred window.

"No, it's not the main thing. It's *the thing.*"

. . .

At exactly 7:01, Jimmy stepped in front of the class, pausing to scan the room. Thirty-two teenage boys sat watching him—all restless, excited, but wary. These young men had seen enough empty promises to last a lifetime. Sara sat near the back, notebook ready, curious how Jimmy would handle a classroom.

Jimmy placed his notes aside and began with a story.

"There was once a young stonecutter named Marcus," he said, "who dreamed of creating a statue so beautiful, so perfect, that people would travel from afar just to gaze upon it. But Marcus was ordinary—no more skilled or talented than anyone else. Still, he decided he would become the kind of craftsman capable of carving such a masterpiece.

"Day after day, Marcus studied, practiced, and endured setbacks. When his hands blistered and his arms ached, he pressed on. When his early sculptures cracked or shattered, he learned patience and precision. With every cut into stone, Marcus was also shaping himself—growing stronger, wiser, more disciplined.

"After years of relentless effort, Marcus unveiled his statue. Crowds gathered, amazed at its flawless beauty. People called him gifted, blessed, a natural genius—but Marcus knew the truth. He *was* great, but no greater than any observer. So what did this goal achiever know that all the spectators didn't?"

Jimmy paused, looking deeply into the eyes watching him.

"The statue wasn't his real achievement," he said quietly. "The true masterpiece was the man he'd cultivated within himself—the man capable of earning his dreams. Marcus hadn't just carved a statue; he'd cultivated his *Power Within.*"

He let the words settle, then added firmly:

"You have the same *Power Within*—it's the strength of character you build that allows you to earn your goals and dreams. That's exactly what this course will help you cultivate."

A few students shifted uneasily, skeptical but curious.

"Look," Jimmy continued, his voice clear and firm. "Here's the uncomfortable truth. Statistics show two-thirds of you could end up right back here in five years if you follow the crowd. But you're not doomed to be a statistic unless you ignore and fail to cultivate your inner power."

A big kid in the back row named Mack spoke up. "What exactly is this '*Power Within*'? Sounds like bullshit to me."

Jimmy studied him for a moment. He knew Mack by reputation as a dangerous character with contempt for authority.

"The *Power Within* is the mental and spiritual force at the center of who you are. It's your inner command center—the part of you that chooses discipline over distraction, purpose over pleasure, and effort over excuses. This power doesn't shout. It waits for you to claim it—through clarity, sacrifice, attention to the right things, and consistent action.

Mack grunted dismissively, and Jimmy wondered why a kid with so much defiance had signed up for an elective course.

He paced slowly, making sure every student felt his sincerity. "Every person has it, but most ignore it. They follow their urges instead of their dreams. But once you activate the *Power Within*, everything changes. You begin to move with direction, speak with authority, and build a life that reflects your highest potential. The world may try to shape you, but when your *Power Within* is alive, you do the shaping. You don't conform."

"I still don't know what the fuck it is!" Mack said.

Jimmy looked at the kid, then silently walked to the

21

podium. "First off, you won't be speaking like that in this class-room. I will speak with respect to you, and you will speak with respect to me. And we will all speak intelligently."

The big kid smirked but said nothing.

With a single sheet of paper in hand, Jimmy returned to the center of the room. "As for better understanding the *Power Within*, maybe this will help," he said. "I want to share a note with you that was given to me by a man who is no longer in this physical world. You may not fully understand this message now, but you will grasp it by the end of this course. I'll read his final words now: it's probably the best explanation I have ever known to describe the essence of the *Power Within*."

> *I am the Silent Power. I speak to you through thought flashes, hunches, inspirations, ideas, compulsions, inclinations, vibrations, and instincts. I am the sixth sense—the repulsion when something isn't quite right, the calmness when it is. I am your inner wisdom, waiting for you to pause and feel me. I am the silence of every day, seeking to guide you.*

> *I am the Unseen Force. I am the coincidence, the lucky break, the chance occurrence that shows up according to your abiding trust. I am the wonder, the marvel, the awe, the life, and the miracle. I am the cooperative energy, and I aid every aspiration according to your daily clarity, strategy, devotion, attention, and faith. I am the Something More you sense. You honor me most by struggling well in the garden.*

As Jimmy finished reading, he looked up. "The man who wrote this message was like a father and mentor to me. He was a master gardener, and the garden was his metaphor for life. It took me a while to understand that this final message was exactly where he wanted me to begin. He asked me to teach this class, and so today we begin with the *Power Within,* or whatever you call this innate force of intelligence that resides in you."

For the next thirty minutes, Jimmy explained the course going forward and the system of a 5-year crusade in general. It was a prosperous lifestyle of repeating good habits, resisting bad habits, working for money, and then working for dreams.

These items in the 5-year crusade system would be tracked and quantified into an objective weekly point score. The challenge of the course was to achieve four weeks in a row at progressive levels of total weekly points. The object of the game was the execution of small efforts for success, which lead to big goals over time.

"You will learn to free the *Power Within,*" Jimmy said in summary, "and give a sacred effort one day at a time."

"So how do we start?" asked Jamal, a boy that Jimmy found intriguing. Blessed with a genius IQ, Jamal was a street hustler who managed an extensive drug trafficking business as a teenager. And now, this young man was asking the same question Jimmy once asked himself when he was incarcerated.

"Where to start?" Jimmy repeated. He then reached into his pocket and pulled out a crumpled piece of paper. "I can speak from my own experience. When my life started falling apart, it was because I had ignored this inner strength. So I wrote something to rebuild myself. It was a daily affirmation—what I called my Crusader's Creed."

He read it slowly to the class, the sacred words clear and powerful, describing a life without self-doubt, self-sabotage, self-neglect, self-delusion, and self-contempt.

Sara watched from the back of the room as he shared his private statement. She had to admit, there was something about him that seemed to connect with these troubled teens. And how he handled the bully with calm strength was effective.

"I repeated this statement every single day," Jimmy said in conclusion. "It wasn't just empty words to me—it became my reality. It rebuilt me from the inside out. The difference between success and failure isn't just about working hard. It's about learning how to cultivate, focus and free your inner power for success. You're born to be great, but you may have to free the greatness within you to know it."

A laid-back, sleepy-looking kid raised his hand. "So all I gotta do is read words to get rich? I'm down for that!"

The other kids chuckled at the remark.

Jimmy grinned. "Words alone never work. Action does. But the right words repeated daily reinforce action. They become your mindset, your identity, your strength. Don't be cynical about affirmations spoken daily to cultivate your inner power."

The sleepy kid shrugged. "Sounds good."

Jimmy chuckled, studying the student, and making a mental note to look into his background. He finished the lesson plan, dismissed the class, and, as he handed out printed copies of the Crusader's Creed, spoke in a serious voice.

"Your first job is to read this every single morning. Not because I say but because you showed up here for a reason. You are the exception in this facility, the rare ones who are going to beat the odds, stay out of jail, better your lives, and thrive in society. You'll start by reading these words daily."

He looked around the room, noting that Jamal stared at the paper longer than the others, like something in it mattered.

"This isn't just another course on goals. It's your personal turning point. It's your crusade. And the transformation begins now, right here, with the power already inside you."

THE CRUSADE WAY

1. Review the Crusader's Creed for 6 minutes daily.
2. Be willing to customize the Crusader's Creed.

CHAPTER 4

Self-Shackles

Self-shackles: self-limiting beliefs,
inner demons, personal issues

Expand your mind until you no longer fit into your current environment. You will then witness that all gardens grow from the mind of the gardener. The way to get a larger garden is to outgrow the one you've got. Set impossible goals, and then apply yourself in your hours to activities that cause an impact for their realization.

— Lessons of the Wealthy Gardener

Jimmy set the lesson plan gently on the table between them. The conference room was quiet; its lighting cast a pale reflection on the window behind Sara. She watched him closely, sensing he was still working through the weight of what he was about to teach. Who was this wealthy guy, exactly?

With the financial freedom to do anything, why did he return to a humble juvenile detention center? More troubling, if she was judging his choice to teach at the facility, what did it say about her own choice to stay at the same institution?

"This lesson's important," Jimmy said, snapping her out of her reverie. "Before we talk about money or habits, daily execution or weekly scorecards, we need to talk about the invisible enemy—the stuff that hinders us from achieving potential."

Sara flipped open the course manual and scanned the bold words listed as separate titles of the Crusader's Creed. "Self-delusion. Self-neglect. Self-sabotage. Self-doubt. Self-contempt."

"That's a lot of self-conflict. What's the plan?"

Jimmy nodded. "Today we'll talk about the internal struggle of success for people who feel stuck, unable to attain their big goals. I try to confine this struggle to just five shackles."

"You think everyone has an internal struggle?"

"Actually, I don't know. What I *do know* is that students can feel stuck and not know why. My job is to increase self-awareness so the boys can identify issues in themselves that they can change. We can't fix what we can't see."

Sara nodded. "I get what you're going for, and I think there's something to it. My concern is, if you focus too much on what's going on inside them, it might feel like you're ignoring everything else they're up against. You know as well as I do—some of these kids are dealing with poverty, unstable homes, violence… the real struggle is more than an inner game."

"True, but if the inner game is lost, all is lost. Success is an inner game first, an outer game second, and the self-shackles are like a five-headed monster that prevents winning either game. These inner demons entangle the *Power Within*."

Sara looked at the manual, then lifted her eyes.

"It's your course," she said. "Just so you know, I'm meeting with the Superintendent every third lesson to review your methods and file an interim report with recommendations."

"Oh really?" Jimmy said. "Recommendations on what?"

"Continuing it or not."

Jimmy almost choked but caught himself. The irony wasn't lost on him—his elective course was being judged against established methods that routinely failed these boys.

"I'll try to impress you then," he said evenly.

"Look, Jimmy, let me be clear. I'm not here to support you—I'm here to protect the boys from you. My job is to make sure your course meets conventional standards."

Jimmy bit his tongue and chose a wise pause. What he wanted to point out but didn't was that her conventional standards led to a 67 percent recidivism rate within five years.

Jimmy nodded without comment. They locked eyes, and then Sara glanced down at the course manual on the table, opened to a page of the Crusader's Creed statement.

"This five-headed monster," she said finally. "These five shackles you talk about defeating. Why not make it visual? Give the boys something they can picture or imagine."

Jimmy realized this was a sign of tacit approval, and he guessed correctly she was offering an olive branch.

He nodded slowly. "An inner monster with five heads? I like that. I can make an image for the classroom lesson."

Sara nodded slowly. For the first time that day, her face softened. Jimmy waited for any extra input from her.

"Alright then," she said. "Let's go slay some monsters."

. ▪ ▪

The room was quiet as Jimmy set down a worn piece of paper on the podium.

"I want to start tonight with a story," he said. "You'll see me start most classes this way. My mentor taught in parables."

The students sat at attention as he scanned the class to gather his thoughts. Sara thought he was being a bit dramatic.

"There was once a man who lived in a village surrounded by mountains," he began, pacing slowly. "The people there told him those mountains were impossible to cross. So he stayed put. He lived a small life and made the best of it. But every night, he dreamed of what might lie beyond."

Jimmy's voice lowered slightly.

"One day, he finally made a decision. He packed food. He studied maps. He rested his body. And when the day came, he set off—determined to begin the journey. But after just a few steps, he felt resistance. The steady pull backward was caused by a stretch cord anchored to a small ring in the ground. It hadn't been noticed before, not until he tried to venture out of his small circle. This stretch cord had been formed by past experiences, early influences, habit patterns, and unchallenged beliefs. He had accepted it all without question."

Jimmy scanned the room.

"The farther he tried to venture away, the more resistance he felt. And when he pushed too far, the cord snapped him back to where he had started. It happened again and again. Over time, he got tired of trying. He learned to live within the small radius the cord allowed. And even though the mountains still called to him, he told himself the dream was unrealistic."

He looked up from the podium.

"Today's lesson is about the invisible cords pulling you backward, keeping you circling the same small life."

He stepped aside as the television screen lit up, displaying a striking image: a lone figure—labeled the *Power Within*—fighting a five-headed monster. Each head was named: Self-delusion, Self-neglect, Self-sabotage, Self-doubt, Self-contempt.

The students stared at the image.

"Who's the dude on the TV wrestling that crazy beast?" one

of them asked. It was the sleepy kid from the last class.

A ripple of laughter moved through the room.

"That dude represents the *Power Within,*" Jimmy said. "He's struggling against a five-headed monster. The five heads are your inner stretch cords—they're demons that make it hard to achieve more than a small life of ordinary achievements."

Jimmy turned and looked at the TV screen.

Self-sabotage

Self-neglect　　Self-doubt

Self-delusion　　Self-contempt

Power Within

"Seriously?" Mack asked. "I signed up for a course on wealth. All you talk about is sculptors, stretch cords, and demons."

The classroom was dead quiet.

"I'll ask you to be patient," Jimmy said. "Tonight, we're not going to talk about how to get rich. We're going to talk about why most people never do. We all possess a great *Power Within,* but not everybody frees their power for success."

He turned to look at the screen, causing all eyes in the room to do the same. Even Sara found herself observing the five-headed monster and the man struggling to be free.

"These are the demons that hold your *Power Within* hostage," Jimmy said. "Once you see them, you can beat them."

He touched his laptop. On the screen, the display zoomed

in on the head of the first demon: **Self-delusion.**

"The first head of the monster is self-delusion," he said. "This one is tricky—because it feels like confidence. It whispers that you're on track, that you have enough time in the future to get around to your goals. When you're older, it will whisper the opposite, telling you that you don't have enough time to reach your goals, that mistakes from your past now prevent your dreams, that you're too old to make big changes."

Jimmy paused. "Self-delusion feels good, but it destroys the *Power Within* because you never face the truth."

Mack grunted. "What's the truth?"

"That you're the only one who believes the excuses and lies you tell yourself. Nobody cares about your reasons for being stuck. You can always improve your habits and efforts. And that's all there is to success. You can change your habits and efforts."

"Easy for you to say."

"Easy for me?" Jimmy repeated. "I was a juvenile delinquent, and my family abandoned me in this place. Never came to visit me once—so don't talk to me about how easy it was for me. I stopped making excuses, and focused on changing me."

The classroom was silent.

Jimmy fixed a level gaze on Mack. "You have a great *Power Within* that can transform everything, but that force is useless until you have the courage to face the reality of your life with honesty, courage, and objective self-awareness."

He touched a key on his laptop, and the TV displayed three questions, which Jimmy read aloud in front of the room.

1. **Do you have big goals or dreams but rarely work 5 to 20 overtime hours every week to earn them?**
2. **Do you believe you're "on the right path" even though**

you lack clear goals for this week, month, and year?

3. **Do you believe you can achieve more than average results without working more than average people?**

Jimmy slowly turned back toward the classroom and then focused again on Mack. "You don't have to answer out loud. But if you said yes to even one of those questions, this demon of self-delusion lives in you. In this course, we'll cut the cord of self-delusion to free your most powerful and essential self."

Mack grunted with disgust, his arms folded tightly. The bully who once assaulted a teacher in a high school cafeteria was displaying his notorious defiance in the classroom.

"You seem to forget," Mack said, "we're in a prison. What the hell can we do in here to achieve money goals?"

"You can increase knowledge," Jimmy said. "It's the first step of all achievement. You can spend hours in the library."

Jamal chuckled. "Mack couldn't find the library."

All the students laughed except Mack, who glared at the back of Jamal's head.

Jimmy continued calmly. "In a crusade, you'll replace self-delusion with a system of accountability that hurts. You'll follow a checklist, and you'll earn a weekly performance score based on execution. Your true effort will show, and some of you will quit because you can't handle the feedback."

He looked at Mack. "I'll teach you a system so clear and simple there's nowhere left to hide—and so you will rise."

Mack didn't speak, but for the first time, he looked away.

Jimmy tapped his laptop again. The screen shifted, zooming in on the second head of the monster: **Self-neglect.**

"This second demon doesn't feel sinister. It doesn't shout— it whispers. It drains your energy, enthusiasm, and strength one day at a time until mild exhaustion feels normal. You begin to accept low energy, irritability, anxiety, or even burnout as part of your personality—not symptoms of neglect. Sometimes it even looks noble, like when you're 'too busy' to care for yourself. But the pain is inevitable: you'll start to feel small and inadequate in the face of a challenging life."

Jimmy scanned the room. "Self-neglect comes in many forms, but I'm talking now about movement. Exercise awakens the big you, restores the *Power Within*, and reduces the small you. It is to the human mind what a reboot is to a computer."

"I gotta exercise to be successful?" a kid asked.

It was the sleepy-looking kid again. Since last class, Jimmy had learned that this student was in juvie due to repeated auto theft.

"What's your name?"

"Slugs," the boy answered.

Jimmy laughed. "Seriously, your nickname is Slugs?"

Slugs nodded with a slight grin.

"No, you don't need to exercise daily to be successful," Jimmy said, "but your success will come easier if you do. You have a great *Power Within* that will help you fulfill your purpose on earth, but a sedentary life weakens this inner force."

"What kind of exercise, and how much?" Slugs asked.

"Those details are for a future lesson plan," Jimmy said. "For now, just know that exercise is not an extra daily ritual to feel good; it's a basic daily requirement to feel normal."

Slugs nodded nonchalantly, and Jimmy leaned down and touched his laptop, causing the TV to display two questions. Jimmy read them aloud, slowly and clearly.

1. **Do you often feel anxious, worried, or irritable without regularly exercising to shift your mental state?**
2. **Do you often feel too busy, drained, or emotionally**

exhausted to exercise for just 15 minutes every day?

Jimmy turned and faced Slugs. "If you answer yes to these questions, the shackle of self-neglect is impairing your *Power Within*. And it means exercising daily would help you rise."

"I thought being tired was just me," Slugs said.

"You're not alone. Very few people exercise daily, even though fifteen minutes would dissolve their stress and restore their best energy. The real problem with a sedentary life is that it feeds on itself: the worse you feel, the less you feel like exercising. It's an avoidable and dangerous downward cycle."

Jimmy shifted his attention from Slugs to scan the entire classroom. "In a crusade, you'll break the self-defeating cycle of a sedentary lifestyle. You'll move your body to dissolve stress and restore your best energy to achieve impossible goals."

The room was still as Jimmy walked across it. He touched the laptop again, causing the TV to shift to a close-up image of the monster's third head: **Self-sabotage.**

"The third demon is self-sabotage," Jimmy said, scanning the classroom. "This demon feels controlling, impulsive, and compulsive. It doesn't listen to reason. It shows its head as an alluring temptation, a distraction from what you're trying to do with your life. When you give in to self-sabotage, you're often rewarded with immediate pleasure. But the pleasure is shallow, fleeting, and often replaced by remorse. The demon will convince you that you lack willpower and discipline."

Jimmy paused. "And that's bullshit. Self-sabotage feels good in the moment, but it enslaves you. It causes your *Power Within* to serve a dark master, one who lurks in the depths of your subconscious mind and opposes your best life."

"You mean drugs and alcohol?" a kid asked.

"Yes, if drugs and alcohol tempt you," Jimmy said, "but it

can be anything that steals your dreams by reducing your focus and effort each day. This demon numbs your mind with constant distraction, drains your power with addiction, and quietly convinces you that harming your future is harmless fun."

He touched a key on his laptop, displaying the next set of questions on the wall-mounted TV, and read them aloud:

1. **Do you often engage in habits or activities that feel good in the moment but waste your time and potential?**
2. **Do you find yourself choosing tension-relieving activities over goal-achieving activities in your free time?**

He paused briefly. "Answer yes even once, and self-sabotage has its hooks in you. Instant gratification can steal your *Power Within* by training your brain to crave comfort instead of work. Over time, you lose the ability to concentrate, choose challenge, or feel fulfilled without constant stimulation."

The kids looked a bit lost, Jimmy thought, and so he decided to make this one personal. "Let me tell you a quick story," he said. "I know a guy who was once in your shoes. He graduated and made a success of his life. It wasn't easy, and he was helped a lot by the guidance of a wise mentor.

"In time, people started to notice him. They called him a winner, a natural, the kind of person who makes success look easy. After a while, the fool started to believe what they said about him, and he started coasting. He stopped doing what had caused his success and started doing things that had nothing to do with his goals—things like watching TV and scrolling on his phone. He even started having several drinks a day.

"Over time, these little acts of self-indulgence became more habitual. Gradually, he lost his drive, motivation, and purpose-driven lifestyle. He lost the *Power Within* that had once fueled his thoughts, motivation, instincts, and purpose."

Jimmy looked around the room.

"I can tell you that self-sabotage kills your full potential, because the fool was me. I fell to self-sabotage and started drifting. It's not always easy to stop drifting, but any vice or bad habit was once learned—and so it can be unlearned."

Jimmy paused, noting that the kids were attentive.

"In a crusade, you will break up with bad habits. You'll abstain from two vices every 30 days. This habit fast restores your focus, your drive, and your will to choose hard work. Most importantly, it frees the *Power Within* for what truly matters."

Jimmy leaned over his laptop and tapped quickly, bringing up two more questions that seemed to surprise the boys.

1. **Do you frequently compare yourself to others, feeling envious as if they have it all together but you don't?**
2. **Do you ever feel overwhelmed by how far away a goal seems, rather than focusing clearly on the next step?**

"If you answered yes to either of those questions, the fourth demon already has you shackled," Jimmy said. "This demon is self-doubt, and it whispers one simple lie: you're not enough. It freezes your feet and convinces you your goals are too big and your skills too weak. It tells you others are better, smarter, luckier, and that you should quit before you embarrass yourself. It makes you cower in a corner when you should be fighting for yourself. It causes the future regret of wondering what might have been if only you had the courage to try."

Jimmy touched his laptop, and the TV showed the fourth head of the monster: **Self-doubt.**

Jimmy noticed Jamal shifting in his seat. "What about you?" he asked. "I get the feeling you've got big plans."

37

"I do, and I ain't going back to jail."

"Care to share your goals?" Jimmy asked.

"Not really. I know what I want."

"Fair enough," Jimmy said, sensing this kid was special. "I'll help you achieve your big plans. In a crusade, you will face self-doubt and respond with action. I will teach you a system of daily action designed not only to control your mindset but also to choose consistent work over worry—because the cure for self-doubt is self-engagement."

Jamal nodded. "Count me in."

Jimmy looked around at the rest of the class. "As for the rest of you, I will deliberately push ambitious goals that you consider unreasonable. When you pursue audacious goals, you will confront the demon of self-doubt. In times of uncertainty, self-doubt will try to convince you that you're smaller than you really are. Self-doubt is a liar. The truth is—you have enough power within you already. You don't need to wait to be better; you just need to move, and stay moving in the right actions."

Jamal smiled as if he understood.

Jimmy smiled back, tapped the laptop one final time, and the last head emerged: **Self-contempt.**

"This final demon," Jimmy said quietly, "might be the worst of them all. It convinces you that you're not worthy. It whispers that you're flawed, broken, not enough—that great things belong to other people, not you. Self-contempt is shame in disguise. It's the reason you'll accept far less than your dreams, and possibly die with a long list of regrets."

He touched his laptop again, and three new questions flashed onto the TV screen behind him. As he looked out over the class, he thought he saw Sara wince. He turned slowly toward the TV and read the questions aloud slowly.

1. Do you criticize yourself more harshly for mistakes than you would criticize a friend for the same thing?
2. When you fall short of a goal or give in to a bad habit, do you question what's wrong with you as a person?
3. Have you stopped believing in miracles for your life, and started resigning yourself to just good enough?

The classroom was motionless.

"Answer yes to even one," Jimmy said softly, "and self-contempt has tricked you into believing lies about yourself. It's the false belief that you're not worthy of the person, place, or situation in your heart of hearts. It's a blindness to an inner power that's so great that it can cause miracles in your life."

He paused. "Truth is, I've fought self-contempt due to killing a person in a drunk driving accident. I've lived with this one. There was a time I questioned whether I deserved to lead this very class—whether I could be more than my past. That's how self-contempt works: it makes you mistake your old identity for your destiny. You forget who you were born to be."

He looked back at the class, his voice firm now.

"The fact is—you are so powerful that even the Universe is on your side. And I'll prove it to you in a 30-Day Expectancy Experiment."

Most of the students seemed to straighten.

"In a crusade, you will unleash your full potential, day in and day out—and there is no gratification greater than knowing that you are the *Power Within*. I will teach you to expect miracles—and then cause them through the power of faith."

Jimmy paused. "Any questions?"

After a long moment, Jimmy touched his computer, and the full image of the five-headed monster reappeared on the

TV, all heads clearly visible with an X over each one.

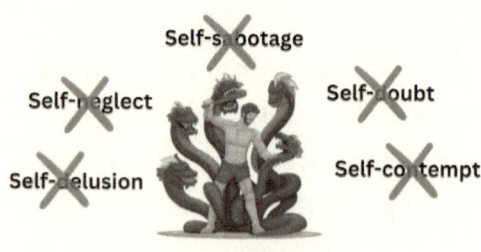

Power Within

"You now know the enemy," Jimmy said. "This struggling man represents the *Power Within,* and this elective course is about breaking your inner shackles to free yourself to achieve every success that you are willing to desire, to expect, and to earn."

For a homework assignment, he passed out a Self-Shackles Questionnaire, a more comprehensive self-assessment than the basic questions he'd asked in the classroom lesson plan.

"If you answer yes to any questions, don't worry—that's exactly what we'll tackle together. Complete this questionnaire honestly. Next week, we start breaking those shackles, one by one, action by action, day by day, hour by hour. In the end, we will free you to experience the life of your impossible dreams."

THE CRUSADE WAY

1. Review the Crusader's Creed for 6 minutes daily.
2. Complete the Self-Shackles Questionnaire.

CHAPTER 5

C *is for* **Clarity**

You are what you do today. Focus on what you want most, why you want it, and what you'll do to earn it.

Decide exactly what you want in your life. I mean exactly what you cannot live without. And then decide the number of weekly hours you're willing to give to this purpose. And finally, fight for these hours as if your life depends on it.

— Lessons of the Wealthy Gardener

Sara pushed open the door to the administrator's lounge and found Jimmy already seated at the table, a tray of food in front of him untouched. He didn't look up. His elbows rested on the table, pencil in hand, eyes fixed on his laptop in front of him.

She set her bag down and raised an eyebrow. "You always this intense before cafeteria meatloaf?"

Jimmy gave a small smile, but it faded quickly.

"I'm always torn between two types of goal setting," he said. "We know that clarity, or focus, is crucial in goal setting, but we don't all agree on what it means. I see the educator's model of goal setting, and the entrepreneur's model of goal setting. And clarity is vastly different in these models.

"I'm not following you."

"Your conventional prison courses on goal achievement recommend the SMART model: make goals that are Specific, Measurable, Achievable, Relevant, and Time-bound. It's a cute little acronym," Jimmy said, "that leads to reasonable goals."

"And what's the alternative?"

"The entrepreneurial model," Jimmy said. "The problem with the SMART method is it lowers goals to reasonable outcomes. It discourages moonshot goals that seem out of reach. We leave the really big goals for those who aren't so smart."

"Big goals are for people like you?" Sara asked in a patronizing tone. She didn't mask her contempt.

Jimmy leaned back and crossed his arms. "Yes, Sara, that's right. Big goals are for dumb people who think like me. I wasn't smart enough to know that wealth was impossible for a juvenile delinquent like me. I wasn't smart enough to know that I should just stay in a job I hated after parole. I wasn't smart enough to accept my role, my status, and my position in life. I was actually so dumb that I chose unreasonable goals and then achieved them."

Sara studied him. His words felt intrusive, almost accusatory. Was he implying her accomplishments were merely 'reasonable,' pedestrian even? Or worse, was he right—had she settled for safety over uncertainty? Was she settling now?

Sara leaned forward. "Why don't we discuss this lesson on clarity. This is the third class: I have a report to write."

Jimmy nodded, sensing a threatening tone. "It's on clarity of purpose. Not the kind people talk about in mission statements or vision boards. I mean daily clarity. The kind that keeps the *Power Within* from scattering into a hundred rays of light."

He tapped the folder in front of him.

"This is a course on moonshot goals, and so mental clarity is more important than what is required for average pursuits."

Sara opened the folder and scanned the outline. "Walk me through it."

"There are four layers of disciplined focus," Jimmy said. "First, the truth no one wants to hear: You are what you do today. Not what you hope, or plan, or say you will do. It's about deeds. You are your choices, your behaviors, your patterns."

"Most people won't like hearing that," Sara said.

"Especially if they're not proud of their daily habits," Jimmy replied. "But it's not judgment. It's a powerful belief, maybe the most important of a 5-year crusade. If what you do today defines you, then every day you choose something different, you start becoming someone new."

Sara nodded. "What's the second layer?"

"Deciding what you want most. One clear, audacious goal. I'll suggest saving $100,000—not because money is the answer to happiness, but because that kind of goal challenges everything they believe about themselves."

Sara tilted her head. "Why not aim for a million?"

He sensed her sarcasm. "I have no problem with thinking big, but some goals are so big they're hard to start. Anyone who wants a million will first need to get $100,000 anyway."

"That's fair," Sara said. "And the third layer?"

"Knowing why you want it," Jimmy said. "If you don't have a strong emotional motive, you'll quit the moment it gets hard. The why has to be stronger than the urge to quit."

"And the fourth layer is tracking?" she asked.

Jimmy nodded. "Tracking your effort makes it visible. It enforces accountability. Tracking is the glue that holds it all together. Tracking causes clarity. If you don't measure what you're doing, you'll never know how much you're doing."

Sara nodded. "Is that where your app comes in?"

"Yeah. It tracks habits, job hours, sacrifices, impact time. It even tracks the habit of tracking," he said, chuckling. "But the boys here can't use an app since they have no phones in juvee. So we'll use the paper scorecard. It's the same system, and the same principles."

"And after parole?"

Jimmy nodded. "That's when the app can be useful for them. But it's just a tool for structure and accountability to win one day at a time. A scorecard serves the same purpose."

Sara studied him, the tray of food still untouched. "You're not just teaching theories, are you? You live these lessons."

Jimmy's voice was steady. "Yes, and I drift when I stop living them. That's the truth I want to pass on. The opposite of clarity isn't confusion—it's just a slow drift without awareness. And once you start drifting, you don't even notice how far you've gone off course until something wakes you up."

■　■　■

Jimmy stood at the front of the room, chalk in hand, and waited for the room to settle. Two seats sat empty—two boys absent meant they'd probably dropped out of the class. He took a breath, focused on the remaining thirty boys, and started with a story.

"Let me tell you a parable," he began.

"We're getting used to it," Slugs joked.

Jimmy grinned. "There was once a young boy who loved the sun. He loved how it warmed his skin, how it made the flowers bloom and brought light to the world. One day, his grandfather handed him a magnifying glass and told him to hold it over a dry leaf. The boy watched as nothing happened. Then the grandfather adjusted the glass, narrowing the beam of sunlight to a single sharp point. It took time, but the boy watched as smoke rose from the leaf, and eventually, it caught fire."

Jimmy paused for a long moment. "The boy was amazed. 'Why didn't it work before?' he asked. The grandfather said, 'Because scattered light warms—but focused light ignites.'"

He scanned the room. "Your *Power Within* is no different. It's your inner light. Spread thin, it keeps you moving, alive, and functional. But focused—it sets you on fire. It turns you into a force that achieves your impossible goals."

He approached the chalkboard and wrote in bold letters:

CLARITY

Jimmy turned toward the class. "Clarity matters because unfocused energy is lost potential. The *Power Within* isn't gone, it's just scattered. Vague goals, weak reasons, distractions, and no structure—these dissipate your inner force. But when you concentrate your energy—when you focus on your goals, your motives, and your daily habits—everything changes. That's how you ignite your *Power Within*. Clarity is the start of every 5-year crusade, and today we'll discuss the four layers."

He turned and wrote on the board:

Step 1
You Are What You DO Today

"You are not your past. You're not your mistakes. You're not even your big wins. You are what you do in the hours of today."

Jamal raised his hand. "Why does it matter?"

"Because it puts the power back in your hands," Jimmy said. "If you eat clean and train like an athlete today—you're an athlete. If you read today—you're a reader. If you scroll for three hours and do nothing—you're a timewaster. And you can change that. Every day, you choose not only who you are in each moment but also who you're becoming."

He looked around the room. "So I want each of you to track what you do this week. Just as an experiment. You don't have to change anything. Just write it down. At the end of seven days, you'll know who you really are now."

Mack cleared his throat. "I already know what I do."

Jimmy studied him. "You'll be shocked when you start tracking. It makes you self-aware. That's clarity. Do with the information what you want, but don't live in self-delusion."

Jimmy returned to the chalkboard and wrote:

Step 2
Focus on What You Want MOST

"Upon parole, you get five years to do as you please," Jimmy said. "What's the one result you'd fight for? What are you willing to suffer for? What's the important mountain in your life?"

A few boys shrugged. A couple looked at the floor. Jimmy walked to the center of the room.

"If you don't know yet, then aim to save $100,000 in five years. I don't care if that's your final goal or not. It's a good start. It's a big goal, it's real, and it forces discipline. You can't luck your way to six figures. You'll need to master this course."

Slugs laughed. "Man, if I had $100,000, I'd be set."

Jimmy grinned. "Set to do what exactly?"

"Start my own auto repair shop."

46

"You might," Jimmy agreed. "But the goal of this course is not just money. It's the transformation. You'll need to master habits, hours, skills, and sacrifice. If you can do that, you can be an entrepreneur."

"I ain't too sure about that!" Slugs objected. "I just want to run my own business and be my own boss."

Jamal sighed aloud. "That's what an entrepreneur does, Slugs."

"Oh, in that case, I'll do that."

There were a few chuckles. Jimmy glanced at Sara, grinned faintly, turned back to the chalkboard, and wrote:

Step 3
Know WHY You Want It

"A clear goal is good," Jimmy said. "But it won't be enough on the days you're tired, frustrated, or overwhelmed. You'll quit unless your reason to win is bigger than your excuse to stop."

He looked directly at Jamal. "What about you? If you had $100,000, what would you do with it?"

Jamal hesitated, then spoke quietly. "I'm not looking to bank money. I want to go to medical school and be a doctor."

A sudden quiet settled over the room. Slugs nodded slowly. Mack rolled his eyes. A few others turned their heads toward Jamal, curious. Sara even seemed to perk up in the back row.

"Why a doctor?" Jimmy asked.

"I saw people die from drugs. I was part of that world. I want to be part of the solution now."

Jimmy nodded. "That's a powerful why."

Jamal added, "And I want to buy my mom a house. Somewhere safe. I don't want her to work another day in her life."

Jimmy let the moment land. "That's what I'm talking about. You won't find that kind of fuel in vague dreams. That's emotional clarity. That's what keeps you moving when it's hard."

He walked to the board again, and wrote:

Step 4
TRACK What You Do

"This is the one layer of clarity people avoid," he said, "but it's where the power is. Tracking your time, habits, actions—brings clarity. It shows you who you're really becoming. It turns vague wishes into data you can work with."

Slugs raised his hand. "What habits and actions?"

"The ones you'll build as we progress through this course. You'll track hours worked, habits completed, sacrifices made, and the number of days you stay consistent. It's not about being perfect. It's about being accountable."

Jimmy looked around the room. "Those of you who change are the ones who tell the truth to yourselves. That's what tracking does. It shows you your truth. And when you know your truth, you can change your direction."

He scanned the room with intensity.

"You are what you do today. Not what you say. Not what you plan. What you do. If you want different results, start doing different things—and keep score. It really is that simple."

For a classroom discussion, Jimmy led the boys through various examples in his own life when he was clear on a goal versus times when he wasn't so clear. He emphasized the importance of reviewing a goal daily, saying it was the simplest ritual with perhaps the highest payoff of all small efforts in the system. He emphasized the importance of not just knowing what you want in the end, but knowing what you will do in the week. A

48

purpose-driven life is about the weekly schedule—especially free hours.

He opened his laptop, and an image appeared on the TV screen: a figure wrestling a five-headed beast. Each head was labeled with a self-shackle. One had an X over it: Self-Delusion.

Power Within

"This is why clarity matters. Most people are trapped by self-delusion—they think they know what they want, think they know why, and think they're doing all they can. But it's not true. They haven't defined their goal clearly. They haven't connected it to a deep motive. And they haven't tracked what they're actually doing. They're deceiving themselves with vague hopes and scattered effort. That's self-delusion."

He touched his laptop and the screen went blank.

"Clarity cuts through that fog. When you know what you want, why you want it, and how you're earning it daily—you're free. You're focused. You're dangerous in a good way. That's how you defeat self-delusion in the modern, distracted age."

Jimmy edited the Self-Delusion section of the Crusader's Creed, customizing it with Jamal's circumstances. Then he read it aloud in front of the class, as Jamal listened intently.

Self-Delusion

Recognizing that it's impossible to achieve audacious goals with vague desires, unclear plans, and a common lifestyle, I defeat the shackle of self-delusion by choosing the easy way of reminding myself what I want most, why I want it, and what I'll do to earn it. <u>I see myself as a medical doctor helping people with health problems; I see my mom living in her dream house and never working another day in her life.</u> To get more than average results, I work more than average people this week. I am defined by what I do, not by what I say I will do. Therefore, I focus on building good habits, taking consistent daily actions, and tracking both my habits and hours to avoid self-deceit. I sacrifice many ordinary things today to do the vital few things that lead to an extraordinary life. I am the kind of person who turns goals into reality through purposeful hours. To prevent the shackle of self-delusion, I know exactly what I want most, I focus on why I want it, and then I track my habits and hours to focus on the process of earning it.

Jimmy finished and looked over the classroom of thirty boys. "The rest of you—make your own version. Say what you want. Say why it matters. And then say how you'll earn it."

THE CRUSADE WAY

1. Revise "Self-Delusion" in the Crusader's Creed.
2. Track what you do in your waking hours for a week.
3. Review the Crusader's Creed for 6 minutes daily.

CHAPTER 6

R *is for* Restore

*Calmness is power. Dissolve your stress and
restore your mind with physical movement.*

We don't need to exercise. We can swing an ax with a dull
blade and still be productive. But if we choose to exercise to
cultivate a daily peak state, our days in the world will be better
because we will be better in the world.

– Lessons of the Wealthy Gardener

Jimmy suggested they "walk and talk" around the track beside
the football field. Sara agreed hesitantly, zipping her jacket
against the chill. The overcast autumn sky and the rhythm of
their footsteps crunching over leaves set a thoughtful pace.

"Tell me about your meeting with the boss," Jimmy said. "I
assume my weekly classes aren't barred since I'm still here."

"I cancelled the meeting," Sara said.

"How come?"

"Because you haven't covered too much material yet. Put
yourself in my shoes, Jimmy. After three weeks, the kids repeat
a six-minute daily affirmation. And, well, that's about all. It's

not wrong to repeat an affirmation each day, but it's not a re-markable thing to report to the administration, is it? And, oh yeah, by the way, I almost forgot. They also completed a ques-tionnaire on self-shackles that points out their flaws. After three classes, that would have been my full progress report."

Jimmy grinned. "It doesn't sound too impressive when you say it like that," he agreed, "but that's just the point. I'm not try-ing to make a complex system of goal achievement. I'm aiming for just the opposite. I want simplicity. I promised a system of getting results that is easier than most people think."

They walked several paces in silence.

"If you told the administration that, after only three classes, the boys learned a practical method to maintain a winning mindset, a ritual that takes six minutes a day, and it will turn them into men who will achieve their dreams, I'll take that re-sult any day. Trust me, this 5-year crusade system will come together in the end. It starts with cultivating the right mindset. It may seem simple now, but I'm not as dumb as you think."

"I doubt you could be," Sara snapped.

Jimmy chuckled. "Every step of this course has a reason, and there's an order for every step. We'll add actionable steps to build and free the *Power Within* starting in today's class."

Sara looked sideways at Jimmy. "Today your lesson is to exercise for success. I still don't fully understand why exercise is so important in your program. We're talking about success and goal-setting—why focus so much on physical exercise?"

Jimmy took a breath. "It's because the first barrier to achieving any goal isn't external—it's internal. It's your state of being. Stress, anxiety, fatigue—they cloud your judgment and weaken your ability to stick with anything long-term. Exercise is the easiest way to reset your mind and restore clarity."

"How exactly?" Sara pressed.

"When you move your body," Jimmy said, "you trigger chemical changes in your brain. Stress hormones decrease. Mood-enhancing chemicals rise. Your brain literally works better after exercise—your thinking becomes sharper, your decisions become clearer, and your emotions become balanced. Exercise puts your *Power Within* back online."

Sara seemed intrigued but unconvinced. "And how much exercise are you going to recommend?"

"Fifteen minutes every day at least," Jimmy answered firmly. "It doesn't need to be intense or complicated. Walking, jogging, cycling—anything that elevates your heart rate consistently. All motion is good, but I personally aim for a face sweat. If my face is sweating, my brain is restoring. That's what I know for sure. It's about activating your mind and spirit."

She frowned thoughtfully. "Every day?"

"No, just on the days when you want to feel good."

■　■　■

Jimmy stood before the boys that evening, his hands resting in his pockets. He waited until the room settled. Two new students, both friends of Jamal's, unexpectedly showed up to the class, evidently based on his recommendation.

"Okay, listen," Jimmy said. "I want you to imagine that you're at your computer, gaming. You're getting dubs and leveling up, when suddenly your device gets slow and laggy. It's running like crap. You pause the game, try everything you can think of to fix the glitch, but nothing's working. It's frustrating because everything is taking so much time in the game due to the slowness of your computer system."

Jimmy began strolling in front of the room. "The last thing you feel like doing is rebooting your device, knowing it will take at least 20 minutes to restart it. But you also know rebooting will return your device to its optimal operating capacity."

Jimmy stopped pacing and looked around the room. "What would you do?"

"I'd reboot it," Slugs said.

Jimmy nodded. "Me too. In fact, not rebooting your computer every morning is the surest way to reduce your productivity during the game. It's neglecting to do what you know is best for you if you want to perform at your highest level."

The kids seemed to agree with the logic.

"The goal of today's lesson is to encourage you to reboot yourself before rushing into your day. Skipping this step in your day is a form of self-neglect. In fact, it's so essential to your *Power Within* that during the challenges at the end of this course, this habit is worth three points, while most others are worth one."

Jimmy looked directly at Slugs.

"If I showed you a morning routine that makes you more efficient in every way—restores your mind, prevents burnout, speeds up your thinking, calms your nerves, reduces impulsive tendencies, improves your sleep, and boosts your overall well-being—would you at least try it for a month?"

"How long's it take?" Slugs asked cautiously.

"Just 15 to 30 minutes a day," Jimmy said.

Slugs hesitated. "Is it hard?"

"Oh, for crying out loud, Slugs!" Jimmy shouted. "If there's one person on this planet who could use an extra shot of daily energy—"

"Okay, I'll do it!" Slugs blurted out. "What I gotta do?"

Jimmy glanced at Sara, who was struggling unsuccessfully to suppress a grin.

"You'll restore your mind with exercise," Jimmy said. "A

workout is to your body what a reboot is to your computer. The easy way to achieve hard goals is to navigate your days with mental clarity, calm energy, and increased focus. Exercise gives you that. It's hard to achieve goals when you're feeling stressed, impulsive, and tired—not in your ideal state of mind."

Jimmy tapped his laptop, and the TV displayed an image of the *Power Within*, surrounded by five inner shackles. There was an X over the shackle of self-neglect.

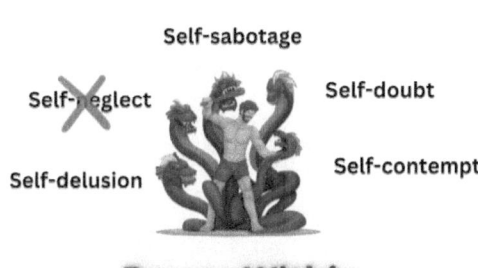

Power Within

"A sedentary day is self-neglect," Jimmy said. "For as long as humans have existed, we have needed to move to stay alive. A caveman who sat on his ass either starved or got beat up by the other cavemen for being a slacker. The truth is that exercise is normal for humans, and it normalizes your mood and energy level. It makes you feel calm and strong because that's how you feel in a natural state. A healthy brain requires movement to function like a healthy brain."

"What kind of exercise?" Slugs asked.

"Any kind," Jimmy shrugged. "When it comes to exercise, you'll feel the biggest payoff in the first 15 minutes, more so than the effect you get between 30 to 60 minutes. So just get moving. What matters is exercising *daily*. To start, just move for 10–15 minutes every day. Get into a routine of daily movement to restore your mind. Take the first step, and keep moving. The goal is to create a daily exercise habit for your brain. I want you to view exercise as a reboot of your body and mind, just like rebooting a computer to make things run faster, cleaner, and more efficiently—every single day."

Mack sneered, "Seriously? Is exercise going to help me save money? In a course on wealth, you're telling me to sweat!"

Jimmy paused briefly, reflecting silently on how his own life had improved after embracing daily exercise, knowing firsthand how transformative this simple habit could be.

"Yes, in a course on wealth building," he said, "or on achieving any other audacious personal dream, I am suggesting you navigate the trials of your mission in your best state of mind."

"Easy peezy," Slugs remarked.

Jimmy touched a button on his laptop. The wall-mounted television displayed a meter labeled "Daily Exercise." The meter consisted of six 10-minute increments. A needle pointed toward the second section, between 10 and 20 minutes.

Daily Exercise

"The optimal amount of exercise is 30 to 60 minutes a day," Jimmy said, "but not everyone has that much time in a 5-year crusade. You'll be busier than most people if you have big goals, so I'd recommend you aim for 15 minutes a day as a minimum. You get the most bang for your buck, in terms of your mental state change. in the first 15 minutes of high intensity exercise. If you choose low intensity exercise, you'll need to go longer."

"But what if I don't have time?" Slugs asked.

The kids chuckled at the question.

"If you don't have 15 minutes, you can exercise for 10 minutes. Studies show that 10 minutes is as effective for mild depression and emotional instability as drugs. The key is to just get into motion—on the treadmill, in the gym, or out the door—without making an 'exercise decision.' The rule is simple: just do something physical every single day until you die."

"What if I don't have 10 minutes?" Slugs persisted.

"If you don't have 10 minutes for exercise, you don't have a life, Slugs. You have the time; you just don't have the priority."

"And exercise earns 3 points daily?" Jamal asked.

Jimmy smiled, encouraged to see the boys already thinking of the weekly point system. He walked them through the simple process of tracking daily exercise, explaining why it earned three points—significantly more than the single point earned for most other habits. He stressed that physical activity was foundational, highlighting how consistent exercise sharpened mental clarity, balanced emotions, and strengthened self-discipline.

As Jimmy described the scoring system, the boys leaned in, their interest visibly growing as they began to grasp how this straightforward daily routine could steadily unlock their potential. They started sharing ideas about finding opportunities to exercise during free periods within the detention center. Jimmy listened carefully, then reminded them to nurture their motivation by embedding clear reasons for exercise into their daily affirmations. He reinforced one final truth: choosing inactivity was not just harmless rest—it was self-neglect, weakening the *Power Within*.

In conclusion, he walked to his desk, picked up a stack of papers, and handed them out.

"These are updated copies of the Crusader's Creed. Look at the section on Self-Neglect, and edit the reasons to exercise."

When they all had a copy, he read the section aloud.

Self-Neglect

Recognizing that it's impossible to achieve audacious goals when I feel tired, overwhelmed, or emotionally off balance, I defeat the shackle of self-neglect by choosing the easy way of daily physical exertion. I am the kind of person who prioritizes health and fitness <u>to strengthen my emotional resilience, mental clarity, and inner drive. A sedentary lifestyle invites burnout, dullness, anxiety, agitation, frustration, fatigue, body fat, and emotional instability</u>. I let no day pass without movement because I know that mood follows motion. When I feel down, I move. When I feel resistance to move, I focus on the first step—the act of starting. On busy days, I choose a short workout over none at all, knowing that exercise consistency matters more than exercise intensity. To avoid the shackle of self-neglect, I move daily to activate my best state of mind.

Jimmy turned back to the group.

"This is now a part of your daily mindset statement, and it will eventually be a part of your mind. You want to remind yourself daily of your motivations for exercise, and the problems of a sedentary life. If your goal is six-pack abs, say that. If your goal is to be smart, write that. If your goal is to lose weight, use it. If your goal is to just feel good, use that motive. The reason doesn't matter as long as you get into movement every day."

"So just five minutes on busy days?" Slugs pressed.

Jimmy rolled his eyes. "Class dismissed. Next class," he said, "we'll talk about resisting the most common vices of modern society that shackle your *Power Within*."

THE CRUSADE WAY

1. Revise "Self-Neglect" in the Crusader's Creed.
2. Review the Crusader's Creed for 6 minutes daily.
3. Exercise 15-to 30 minutes every day until you die.

CHAPTER 7

U *is for* Unlearn

Your vices are just habits that feel good but
harm you. Unlearn your vices with a habit fast.

Prosperity is a way of life built on doing the right things. The longer we do the right things, the more these right things become our habitual patterns. It's not that habits lead to effortless achievement, but that our most repeated activities—over time—will become almost involuntary. Habits compel us, and then they eventually control us.

– Lessons of the Wealthy Gardener

Sara left the meeting with the Superintendent in a state of frustration and resignation. It was a sickening feeling in the pit of her stomach that she'd felt too many times in the past three years. She'd taken great pains to assemble a proper report of the class that explained in detail the concept of the *Power Within*, how it could be shackled by common self-limitations, and why each lesson plan so far was meant to address these self-shackles.

When it was over, she knew for sure that the Superintendent didn't really care about this weekly extracurricular course, the

61

breakdown of lessons, or whether it was continued. He had the air of a busy man who considered the meeting a small annoyance in his more important responsibilities. It was always this way at the facility: she was ignored and overlooked in a system that was focused on maintaining order while failing the boys.

Sitting in her car after work, Sara realized that she'd had the same condescending attitude toward Jimmy and the course. He was trying his best to offer a new approach, and she was receiving it as if this class was a weekly annoyance in her important responsibilities. Sara felt privately ashamed, but the realization caused her to take a surprising action.

On an impulsive whim, she downloaded the tracking app. It felt absurd, yet she was tired—deeply tired—of feeling powerless. What was she doing? Had Jimmy gotten under her skin? She found the Audios page and listened to the full Crusader's Creed recording with an open mind for the first time. She replayed it again and again on her drive home.

What did she have to lose? Sara knew she was stuck in a job that paid the bills but robbed her of joy and wasted her full potential. What harm could come from checking out this dumb app and evaluating it as part of her role to oversee the course?

For the next two days, during her commute, she listened to the Crusader's Creed. On the third day, she took the extra step of customizing her own recording, setting a goal for meaningful social work with higher pay. If she could achieve those two goals, it would be a miracle! She vowed to try the crusade life while not telling a soul. Nobody needed to know her secret.

At the usual hour, Sara sat across from Jimmy in the reformatory conference room, an open folder on the table between them. Sara flipped through the course outline, then looked up. She had no plans of giving him the satisfaction of her crusade experiment. And he seemed to be focused on the lesson.

"How did the progress report go?" Jimmy asked.

"The meeting went fine," she said dismissively. "We're scheduled to meet again, after the next three classes, and my boss warned me that there'd better be more actionable steps to this course, or he will cut it himself."

Jimmy's eyes flashed with anger, but he remained silent long enough to regain his composure. It baffled him how these institutions disregarded new methods while protecting their traditional ways that were clearly failing the incarcerated boys.

Finally he said, "I'll keep that in mind."

Sara nodded. "I read your lesson on unlearning habits. Tell me why these so-called 'bad habits' matter so much. How exactly do they prevent success and weaken the *Power Within?*"

Jimmy leaned forward, trying to figure out what was different about her today. "Do you recall the first lesson when I told the kids they were like the sculptors, and the masterpiece was not what they'd get in the end but who they'd become?"

"Of course."

"Bad habits and vices play a big role in who they become. They don't just waste time," he said. "They also dull the brain."

Sara narrowed her eyes slightly. "How exactly?"

"Things like endless scrolling, binge-watching shows, junk food, video games—these behaviors deliver quick hits of pleasure," he said. "They feel good in the moment, but harm you in the long run. Over time, they hijack your brain's reward system. They drain your energy, blur your focus, and weaken your ability to control your impulses. When your dopamine system gets overloaded, real life starts to feel dull, boring, and unfulfilling by comparison."

"And so bad habits become addictions," Sara said, "and these addictions weaken the *Power Within*. Is this the point?"

"Yes, because they affect the brain on a biological level that impairs it. When you indulge in these habits regularly, your brain craves more stimulation. Your tolerance for stress decreases, and your patience and willpower fade. Achieving any meaningful goal requires sustained effort, but when your brain constantly seeks instant gratification, due to its impaired state, your ability to stay consistent and disciplined breaks down."

Sara nodded slowly, processing. "And that's why you recommend this 'habit fast'?"

"Yes. It's essential," Jimmy said firmly. "The habit fast is a deliberate, temporary break from your most distracting habits — for just thirty days. The reason for it is to reset your dopamine system, regain clarity, and restore your self-control to normal."

"How does that reset happen?" Sara asked skeptically.

Jimmy leaned forward. "It's simple biology. When you stop feeding your brain constant dopamine hits, your reward system starts to rebalance. After about two weeks, most people begin noticing significant changes. They feel calmer, clearer, more energetic. Their cravings fade, sleep improves, anxiety reduces, and motivation returns. Most importantly, their sense of self-control strengthens dramatically."

Sara considered this, thinking of her own repetitive habits as well as the bad habits of juvenile delinquents. "What kind of habits do you typically recommend cutting?"

Jimmy opened the manual and pointed to a list:

- Social media scrolling
- Online shopping
- Binge-watching TV
- Junk food or mindless snacking
- Gambling
- Alcohol or drugs
- Constant smartphone checking

- Excessive gaming
- Pornography

"These behaviors aren't just distracting," Jimmy emphasized. "They directly undermine your inner power. They create internal resistance. When your inner state is scattered, anxious, or addicted to quick pleasure, you lose the clarity and discipline needed for meaningful progress."

Sara leaned back, thoughtful. "And you track bad habits?"

"Yes," he said, opening the app on his phone. "The system is structured around accountability. Tracking keeps it real. You choose two habits to eliminate for thirty days. Each day you abstain, you get no points. But if you slip, you lose points. It's a subtle but powerful form of negative reinforcement. Every decision counts. Over time, you see the direct impact that your habits have on your energy, focus, and discipline."

Sara nodded thoughtfully. "Why not give positive points for avoiding a habit? It seems more supportive to earn points."

"I wanted the system to mimic goal achievement in real life," Jimmy said. "We don't earn great things by avoiding bad habits, but rather, we lose ability to achieve great things. And big picture, we impair the strength of the *Power Within.*"

Sara sighed. "I don't like it, but I can see your point. You also recommend meditation in a lesson about bad habits—why?"

"Meditation is known to rebalance the dopamine pathways in your brain. It's the easy way to supercharge the dopamine reset during the habit fast. More than that, meditation is a way to connect with spirituality, and spiritual well-being is a key factor in breaking bad habits. I don't expect you to support it."

Sara was taken aback. "Why?

"You've made it clear that you're not quite sold on the *Power Within.* I figure you just believe in things you can see."

Sara looked serious. "It's my job to challenge your theories in the course. That doesn't make me a materialist. We allow the 12-Step program in our institution to help the boys break addictions," Sara said. "It's a double standard to allow spirituality for one course while not supporting the same principles for another course. That said, I will report that a meditation practice is about reclaiming power by normalizing brain chemistry."

Jimmy paused. "Exactly. Bad habits don't just waste your time—they weaken your inner strength. Breaking free from them restores your *Power Within*. With that inner strength restored, success and clarity follow naturally. Life just gets easier."

■　■　■

Jimmy stood beside the podium, waiting for everyone to take their seat. Two more students entered the classroom unannounced this evening. He looked out at the group, not as a room full of troublemakers, but as young men shaped by a thousand forces—peer pressure, family history, cultural bias, inherited disadvantage, and survival habits formed too early. He saw what others might overlook: possibility. These weren't broken kids. These were untrained minds. And tonight, they would confront one of the most important truths of the entire crusade.

At 7 sharp, he stepped forward and waited for silence.

"Tonight's lesson is about temptation," Jimmy said. "Not the kind that shows up once in a while—but the kind that visits you every single day. The kind that feels harmless but eats away at your strength, discipline, and the *Power Within*."

He walked slowly along the front row.

"I want you to imagine your 5-year crusade like a mountain. You reach the summit with small, steady steps. It's slow, it's daily, and you eventually learn to trust the process."

He paused.

"Now imagine you're literally climbing that mountain. Day after day, you push forward. But your legs are getting sore from the effort. To help the pain, you apply a muscle cream. It soothes the soreness, so you do it again the next day. And the next."

He moved back to the center of the room.

"After a while, it becomes routine. You apply the cream in the morning, after lunch, and before bed. Rubbing it in feels good. It becomes your little pleasure. But one day, another climber sees what you're doing and stops. He tells you something that shocks you: the cream is the reason your legs are hurting. It's not fixing the soreness, he claims, but causing it."

Jimmy looked around the room.

"He says if you stop using the cream, your muscles will heal naturally. You'll stop hurting. You'll get stronger again. Now let me ask you—if you were that climber, what would you do?"

Slugs raised a hand. "I'd stop using the cream."

"Exactly," Jimmy said. "Even if it was hard to quit at first, you'd stop. Because you realize the thing that felt good was actually making the climb harder."

He let the idea settle.

"To win big goals in a 5-year crusade, you need to stop doing things that feel good in the moment but harm you in the long run. I'm talking about vices and temptations. They feel good. They feel harmless. But they quietly rob you of your strength. They numb your mind, drain your energy, and take away your inner power. And you don't even notice until you're stuck."

Jimmy turned to his laptop and tapped a key. The TV screen behind him lit up with a diagram of a human brain, surrounded by three arrows in a cycle: Try → Suffer → Rise.

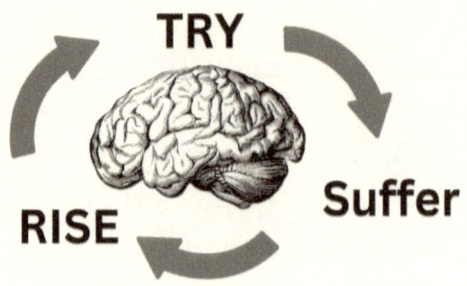

"This is the cycle of change. First, you try to break the habit. Then you suffer for a while—usually two weeks. But if you push through it, you rise. Your brain starts to heal. Your energy returns. You begin to feel like yourself again."

He paused. "It's a predictable cycle due to the brain's dopamine reset. You'll feel better without the dopamine."

"We got dope in our brains?" Slugs wisecracked.

Jimmy smiled. "You've got dopamine. It's a brain chemical. It rewards you for doing something meaningful. When you finish a workout or hit a goal, your brain gives you a hit of dopamine. It motivates you to do it again."

He stepped to the chalkboard and wrote:

The Modern Trap: Feeling Good Fast

"But here's the problem. Some things—like junk food, social media, weed, vaping, gaming—give you a huge hit of dopamine for almost no effort. That confuses your brain. It wasn't built to handle that much dopamine, and surely not that fast of a hit. So it adapts by shutting down dopamine receptors."

He looked back at the group. "That's why you start feeling numb. That's why you lose motivation. That's why your regular life seems dull and boring. You're overstimulated. And it takes more and more of the habit to feel anything at all."

Jimmy turned and wrote on the board again:

More Cravings, Less Control

"Soon, you're not in charge anymore. The habit soon has you in its grip. You scroll longer, eat more, escape more, but it doesn't satisfy you as much as it once did. And while you're busy chasing those hits, your goals are getting buried. Your *Power Within* fades because your self-control is being hijacked."

He paused. "But there's good news. You can get it back."

Jimmy turned to the chalkboard and wrote:

Train the Brain to Want the Right Things

"Your brain is plastic. That means it changes. When you stop feeding it empty dopamine, it begins to heal. When you stop bad habits, it gets healthy. After a few weeks, your motivation starts coming from the right things—effort, progress, achievement. That's when the *Power Within* begins to rise again."

Slugs frowned. "Doing hard stuff can feel good?"

Jimmy nodded. "That's exactly right. You weren't made to scroll and zone out all day. You weren't made for a relaxed, idle life. You were built to grow. And when you grow, it feels good. That's real dopamine—earned by satisfying daily efforts."

He turned and wrote on the chalkboard:

Habit Fast + Meditation

"For the next thirty days, cut two bad habits. Cold turkey. No tapering, no excuses. Total abstinence. It might be sugar. It might be gossip. It might be gambling, cussing, or fighting. Whatever you do that tends to be compulsive and impulsive—drop it."

Mack laughed out loud. "We're in a prison."

"That detail has not escaped me," Jimmy quipped.

"What the fuck can we give up in a prison?"

Jimmy walked silently down the aisle and stopped three feet from Mack. "I warned you once about how we talk in this class. That's strike two. One more strike, and you're out the door."

Mack seemed ready to stand but then backed down.

Jimmy remained still. "Learn to control your temper, Mack. Channel your power," he said calmly. "If you use it, you'll be unstoppable. But if you allow it to use you, you'll be back in jail."

Mack nodded in response to the advice.

"You all have vices," Jimmy said, returning to the front of the room. "You still have escape patterns. You still know when you're wasting time, picking fights, or gambling. Cut two vices. You know what they are."

He approached the chalkboard and wrote:

Meditate for Faster Recovery

"You'll also meditate every day. Five, ten, or fifteen minutes. Just sit. No noise, no distraction. Just empty your mind. Be still. It gets easier with practice, but only for those who stay with it. Your focus will sharpen. Your concentration will grow."

Slugs chuckled. "I can be still and do nothing."

"It's not as easy as you think," Jimmy said.

"I can't imagine anything easier than doing nothing."

Mack spoke up. "What if I just want to get rich?"

Jimmy looked at him. "How rich do you want to get?"

"I'd be happy with a million," Mack said.

"It will take more than meditation," Jimmy said, "but meditation won't hurt your chances. A meditation practice will help you stay centered for productive days. I'm not asking you to sit for long—just five, ten, or fifteen minutes a day to strengthen your brain. It's a quick daily habit. And the harder it is for you to sit in a silent room, the more your brain needs you to do it."

Jamal chuckled. "Mack needs a lot of sitting."

All the boys laughed, except Mack.

"Meditation turbocharges the dopamine reset," Jimmy said. "And that's the reason to do it. It helps fix your dopamine."

Jamal raised a hand. "So dopamine isn't bad?"

"Not at all," Jimmy said. "It's just a messenger chemical. It tells your brain what's worth chasing. You're the one who trains it. If you chase junk, it'll keep asking for junk. If you start chasing progress, your brain will adjust. And that's when your *Power Within* comes alive."

He tapped the laptop. The TV showed an image of the *Power Within* surrounded by five shackles. One—Self-Sabotage—was marked with an X.

Power Within

"The surest way to fail is to keep doing what feels good but weakens you. The easiest way to win goals is to stop vices and bad habits. You don't need more willpower. You need fewer temptations. Do a 30-day habit fast. That's how you start to rise."

He turned to Jamal. "Why is checking your phone—or

whatever you use to escape—a real threat to your future?"

Jamal answered, "Because it steals your ability to concentrate. And you need focus to do anything great."

"Exactly," Jimmy said. "And most people give up their focus without a fight."

He looked at Slugs. "Why should you resist the TV or whatever numbs you every night?"

"To not waste time?" Slugs guessed.

Jimmy nodded. "Yes—but its deeper than that. Constant entertainment rewires your brain to crave shallow pleasure. You get overly stimulated and it starts to feel normal. Once that happens, deep effort begins to feel impossible. That's the real cost.

"Now let's review the Crusader's Creed and customize it with two vices that you may want to break up with for 30-days."

He clicked a tab on his laptop. The screen displayed the "Self-Sabotage" section of in Crusader's Creed statement, which he read aloud as the boys listened attentively.

Self-Sabotage

Recognizing that it's impossible to achieve audacious goals while I'm held back by nonbeneficial habits and vices, I defeat the shackle of self-sabotage by choosing the easy way of eliminating temptations that don't align with my goals. <u>I abstain from junk food and TV at this juvenile detention center. I avoid these vices to experience more self-discipline, concentration, and productivity</u>. I am the kind of person who lives freely, without the weight of self-sabotaging behaviors, vices, or socially accepted addictions. I reject anything that feels good in the moment but harms me in the long run. To break the grip of unwanted habits that are not aligned with my highest purpose, I commit to a habit fast plus a daily *meditation to recondition my brain for peak performance.*

Jimmy turned to face the boys. "This week, revise your Crusader's Creed. Choose your two bad habits. Start your daily meditation. This is how you clear space—for clarity, for focus, and for purpose. This is how you free your *Power Within.*"

Jimmy dismissed the class. As they stood to leave, he handed each student a homework sheet.

"Next class," he said, "we'll move from building your power to engaging it. But it all starts here. Freeing yourself from what weakens you is how you access what strengthens you."

THE CRUSADE WAY

1. Revise "Self-Sabotage" in the Crusader's Creed.
2. Review the Crusader's Creed for 6 minutes daily.
3. Exercise for 15-30 minutes every day until you die.
4. Abstain from 2 vices for the 30-day habit fast.
5. Meditate for 5, 10, or 15 minutes once a day.

Part Two
Self-Engagement

CHAPTER 8

S *is for* Sacrifice

An extraordinary life requires the sacrifice
of ordinary things. Sacrifice the many ordinary
things that matter least to your goals.

We pay the price of an extraordinary life, or we pay the regrets
of an average life. An extraordinary life requires a sacrifice of
our leisure hours, but an ordinary life requires a sacrifice of
our dreams. It depends on what is most wanted in the garden.
– Lessons of the Wealthy Gardener

During the week, Sara resumed her normal life while adhering
to just a couple new daily disciplines, which she secretly
tracked on the app. She listened to her customized Crusader's
Creed, prioritized tasks, and abstained from both Instagram
and television. It didn't require much sacrifice to do these small
things; in fact, the change was so slight that nobody noticed.

Within herself, however, Sara realized she felt better in an
indescribable way. Jimmy would call it the *Power Within*, and
that was a good reason to keep it a secret from him! She tracked
her small efforts on the app, which calculated sixteen points on

most days. If she slipped on a bad habit (checking Instagram, for example), a point was subtracted from this total. The scoring system made tracking fun.

What was not so fun, however, was her growing dissatisfaction with her present life conditions. Could it be that the *Power Within* was causing a sense of discord? Did clarity make her more aware of the discontent she felt deep inside? She wasn't sure why her life felt more misaligned, but it just did.

Sara opened the door and entered the conference room, where Jimmy was sitting and waiting. He seemed to study her longer than normal, she thought, as if he sensed something. Her suspicion didn't last, as he quickly got down to business.

"A crusade is a temporary *sacrifice*," he said, "for a permanent result. That's the core of it. But getting young people to sacrifice—even for their own good—is the hardest part of this program."

Sara gave a skeptical smile. "Sacrifice? Half the time, we can't even get them to show up for kitchen duty, let alone hold down a job."

"That kind of goal is part of the problem," Jimmy said. "There's nothing exciting about holding down a job just to survive. But if they have something bold to aim for—something meaningful—then sacrifice starts to make sense. A 5-year plan to save $100,000 is a moonshot goal for most of these boys, and I hope that's exactly why it will motivate them to sacrifice."

Sara twirled a pencil. "What's the sacrifice of a crusade?"

"The sacrifice of a crusade depends on the size of the end goal. For most goals, the sacrifice is 5 to 20 free hours every week to do the extra work of a crusade. The bigger the goal, the bigger the sacrifice. The bigger the prize, the bigger the price. Take you, for example. You have several degrees, right?"

Sara nodded warily. "I have three, yes."

"How was it possible for you to graduate with a bachelor's degree in three years of college, and then work a full-time job, handle the duties of being a single mother, and earn two additional master's degrees in your twenties?"

Sara almost fell over. "How do you know about me?"

"You have authority to shut down this course," Jimmy said. "It's my job to know about you. I asked around, and your history is easily researched. I have to say, Sara, you're pretty impressive on paper. I don't know how you did it. Your achievements tell me you are not only smarter than nearly anyone I know, but you can outwork an army."

She looked at him speechlessly.

"So let's talk about sacrifices. How did you do it?"

"I used every minute," Sara said quietly. "And I lost a lot of sleep. I had help with my daughter, and I wasn't always there for her. One of my beefs with self-help is that it all seems so fun, and people don't emphasize the work and sacrifice."

Jimmy nodded. "Goals take an emotional toll. We need to sacrifice hobbies, pleasures, sleep, and even relationships."

"And you'll be honest about it in the course?"

"Absolutely. And if the goal is financial, we need to accept financial sacrifices on top of that load. It's a lot to ask."

Sara nodded slowly. "What about your sacrifices?"

"To achieve financial success, you mean?"

"Yes, of course."

Jimmy sighed audibly. "Where to begin? I basically worked, exercised, and slept. If I wasn't working or sleeping, I was thinking about strategies. I didn't have friends except for a few colleagues. I didn't have any hobbies. I pretty much lived a purpose-driven life with no balance whatsoever, but I liked it."

Sara thought a moment. "You didn't date?"

"No, I didn't date."

"That's a lot of sacrifice," she said.

"Is it though?" Jimmy asked. "The greatest challenge was doing all that work in the face of uncertainty. I was never sure it was all going to work out. I needed to work in those free hours with no promise of payoff."

Sara nodded. "And you needed to sacrifice many things that people take for granted, things they even feel are necessary, to make time for work," she said. "The evenings and weekends are the battleground of extraordinary goals."

Jimmy looked at her with admiration. They locked eyes in a moment of shared understanding, but then he looked away.

"You can't reach extraordinary goals," he said, "if you spend all your free time doing ordinary things. When you waste time, you waste your potential. The *Power Within* requires time spent in vital engagements. Without sacrifice, it remains trapped. With sacrifices, there's time to achieve. I chose to go after my goals at any cost, even if I had to do it alone."

Sara paused and leaned in with an intense look in her eyes. "I heard that about you," she said. "People say that you're a contented loner. Is that why you have no family?"

Jimmy felt the blood rush to his face. "How do you know about that?"

"It's my job to know about the developer of a course in my juvenile detention center. You either hatched from an egg, or you're estranged from your family. I assumed the latter."

Jimmy leaned back in his chair. "I was raised in a strict family with religious values. When I killed a woman on my sixteenth birthday in a drunk-driving accident, do you know how often my family visited me at the juvenile detention center?"

Sara breathed. "No, I don't know."

"Well, let me help you. Zero. They never came to visit me, not once, when I was young, alone, and in a prison. I met a man who took me under his wing, and he became my father."

Sara swallowed. "They haven't contacted you since?"

"Yes, they've tried. But you know what? They weren't there for me when I needed them, and now I don't need them."

. . .

Jimmy stood at the front of the classroom, quiet, waiting for every boy to settle in. He noticed another new kid straggle in alone at the very last moment. He glanced at Sara and shrugged; she simply shrugged back, as if to say, *Go with the flow*. He finally began—not with a lecture, but with a story.

"There was once a woman who inherited a house on the edge of a beautiful cliff," Jimmy said, pacing slowly. "It needed some modest renovations, but the view was breathtaking. From her porch, she could see the ocean stretching forever. Inside, the house was strong but bare—empty walls, no furniture, no warmth. She told herself she'd make it a dream home, but first, she just wanted to enjoy it. After all, she worked a regular forty-hour job."

He paused.

"Each morning she stood on that porch and promised she'd start the hard work tomorrow. But the cliff air was so fresh. The sunrises were so beautiful. So instead, she hosted brunches. She invited friends to enjoy the view. She filled her time with pleasant distractions—walks, naps, wine, reading. Weeks turned into months. Then years. The house remained unfinished and unrepaired. Cracks formed. The porch sagged. The roof started to leak. Still, she said, 'I have so little time. I deserve balance.'"

Jimmy let the silence sit.

"By the time she was ready to renovate, the roof had rotted. The foundation had eroded. Her chance had passed. The dream was gone, and so was her great future in the house on the cliff."

He looked around the room.

"The moral of the story: if you never give your dream what it asks for, it walks away—not all at once, but piece by piece. A balanced life can feel right, but it often provides today's comfort at the expense of tomorrow's regret."

Jimmy touched his laptop, and the TV displayed a quote:

**An extraordinary life requires the sacrifice
of your leisure hours, but an ordinary life
requires the sacrifice of your dreams.**

He turned back to the class. "Today is about the sacrifice of a 5-year crusade. I want it to be very clear to you that you will sacrifice in your life. You will sacrifice time today, or you will sacrifice achievements in the future. There is no getting around this immutable reality: you will sacrifice in a five-year crusade. And the sacrifice is 5 to 20 hours a week for a better future."

He touched a key on his laptop, and the TV displayed a weekly schedule. Four weekly slots were circled to designate the opportunity to work on important goals in free time.

Weekdays (x5)	Weekends (x2)
Morning routine	Morning routine
Job	◯
Lunch	Lunch
Job	◯
Dinner	Dinner
◯	◯

"Take a long look at this schedule. These four time slots

represent your opportunity to achieve goals with extra hours. Early mornings. Late evenings. Weekend blocks. You have about 60 hours available in these time slots. You'll claim some of these hours to use your full potential and engage the *Power Within*."

"Doing what?" Slugs asked.

"Doing high impact activities that are goal-achieving," Jimmy replied. "You will do what matters most for your goals and sacrifice what matters least for your goals. We'll talk about the sacrifice today. Let's dig into your own lives now. On a sheet of paper, write your five-year goal clearly at the top."

The boys quickly took out their notebooks. He waited until they seemed to all be done writing.

"Draw a horizontal line across the middle," Jimmy continued, "and below that line, list every single activity you regularly did before you got into trouble—activities that filled your mornings, evenings, or weekends. Be honest with yourself. Every detail counts. Every hour matters. Make a list."

The room quieted to thoughtful murmurs as each boy began writing. Jimmy walked slowly among the desks, watching closely. Jamal scribbled intently, Slugs hesitated, glancing at others' papers for inspiration, while Mack listed items quickly, chuckling arrogantly at some of his own admissions.

After ten minutes, Jimmy called for attention. "Now, look at your paper. Everything you listed below the line is competing directly with your goal above it. This isn't theory—it's real life. Your goal demands your time, or it will be *swept away* by time. Your task is to identify clearly how you can reclaim 5 to 20 hours a week by trimming back these comfort activities."

The boys were staring at the papers on their desks.

"Alright, let's talk about what you've written. Who wants to start?"

Slugs raised a hand. "Mainly video games, scrolling on social media, stealing cars. And sleeping in as long as possible. I'm not sure what I was always doing besides those things."

The classroom rippled with laughter.

"Good honesty, Slugs," Jimmy acknowledged. "I get that completely, except the car stealing part. When I first did a time audit, I was at a loss for what consumed all of my free time."

Jimmy glanced to the back of the room. "How about you, Mack?"

Mack sighed, leaning back casually. "A lot of hanging out—partying, getting in fights, listening to music, chasing girls."

"Thanks, Mack," Jimmy said. "You can forget most of that stuff in the next five years if you want to achieve big goals."

"We'll see about that," Mack said.

Jimmy shrugged nonchalantly, although he was starting to get an ominous feeling about this character. He tried to conceal his perception, and looked at Jamal. "What about your list?"

Jamal straightened. "I was a businessman. When I wasn't in school, I worked on my side hustle. That's all it was for me."

"Excellent," Jimmy nodded. "And when you're discharged, you can redirect that same energy to your new goal of becoming a doctor. You picked a profession that requires a huge amount of sacrifice, probably ten years of your life in exchange for it. Are you willing to accept that much struggle?"

"I gotta be doing something," Jamal shrugged. "I might as well be doing something that gets me what I want."

"We're always doing something," Jimmy agreed. "And the quality of our free hours is the main difference between success and failure in our adult life. Let's make the sacrifice of a crusade really simple. You're going to work 40 hours at a job. Your commute to work uses hours on top of the workdays. You'll also have unavoidable chores around the house. So now you have maybe fifty weekly hours to do as you please."

Jimmy strolled to the center of the room.

"And if you're not careful," he said, "you can become just like the woman who inherited a house on the edge of a cliff. You will think you deserve some balance, and you'll be tempted to rest. You'll be tired, so you'll choose passivity. You will be tempted to put off the sacrifice of real work until next week, always procrastinating because you're too busy doing pleasurable things. And before you know it, your dream is gone. It slips away in time, because you gave it no attention. Let me show you exactly where most dreams go to die."

Jimmy touched a key on his laptop, and the TV behind him displayed a list labeled "Where Your Dreams Go to Die." He turned and read the list aloud, slowly and emphatically.

Where Your Dreams Go to Die

- Watching TV & Streaming Shows (18 hours/week)
- Mobile Phone & Social Media (23 hours/week)
- Video Games & Online Browsing (6 hours/week)
- Socializing & Hanging Out (4–7 hours/week)
- Sports, Exercise & Recreation (3–5 hours/week)
- Sleeping Extra & Naps (4–6 hours/week)
- Shopping & Unnecessary Spending (2–3 hours/week)

Jimmy turned. "This is where attention goes for everyday adults in society during non-working hours. It's also where your *Power Within* goes when you don't sacrifice ordinary things. You'll either sacrifice these things, or you'll sacrifice your dreams. If you want an extraordinary life, you need to cut back or eliminate a lot of ordinary, mindless things."

He tapped his laptop again. The TV displayed an image of the *Power Within* surrounded by five shackles. An X covered the shackle labeled "Self-Delusion."

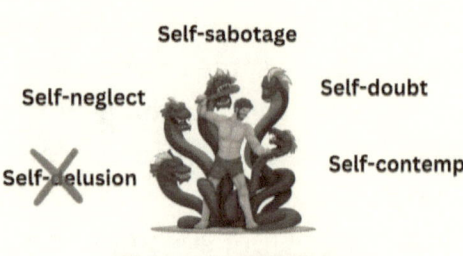

Power Within

"It's self-delusion to expect an extraordinary life while you give all your free time to ordinary things," Jimmy said. "Every ordinary pleasure you sacrifice today helps you reclaim weekly hours for your future—and for your *Power Within* to shine. Sacrifice what matters least for goals to do what matters most."

Jimmy paused, waiting for questions.

"Can anyone guess the homework?" he asked.

Mack chuckled. "Revise the brainwashing statement?"

"Not this time," Jimmy said. "You'll clear 5 to 20 hours this week for effort beyond your regular job. Next week, we'll discuss exactly how to use those reclaimed hours. Remember, every hour is another brick in the foundation of your dream. Don't let your future slip away like the house on the cliff."

Jimmy looked a Mack for a long moment, and then scanned the room before passing out the homework assignment. The Crusade Way was a growing list that consisted of repeating good habits and resisting poor behaviors.

"The next lesson," he said, "is the most important. We'll talk about impact hours, and the activity that earns goals."

86

THE CRUSADE WAY

1. Review the Crusader's Creed for 6 minutes daily.
2. Exercise for 10-20 minutes every day until you die.
3. Abstain from 2 vices for the 30-day habit fast.
4. Meditate for 5, 10, or 15 minutes once a day.
5. Clear 5 to 20 hours this week for efforts.

CHAPTER 9

A *is for* Activity

Doing the right thing is more important than
doing things right. Prioritize the vital few things
that matter most to your goals.

I ascribe these results to doing the right things and doing them consistently. I committed myself to make room for more impact activities. I revamped my weekly schedule, avoiding hollow hours to better use the days.

– Lessons of the Wealthy Gardener

During the week, Sara added meditation to her growing list of small efforts repeated day in and day out; her point total averaged 17 on weekdays. She noticed that without Instagram and television, her legendary memory and concentration were returning. With these daily habit fasts, she sensed more free time. More importantly, she had more quality time with her daughter, Faith. Lastly, Sara was becoming increasingly annoyed with the men in her life—those at work and the one at home. Faith's dad lived with them for convenience, and as she walked to the meeting, she thought he just had to go.

She joined Jimmy at the usual conference table, and within minutes they were deep in a discussion about Sara's final review of the course to the administration.

"At this point," Sara complained, "I may see value in your course, but you already know my boss is not in favor of it."

Jimmy sighed. "What's up his ass anyway?"

"He dislikes your *Power Within* concept," Sara said. "I think he's an atheist, or a materialist, and he's against it."

Jimmy considered the situation. "I think you'll be okay going into this meeting. I mean, you can tell them I taught the boys how to achieve a prosperous lifestyle by controlling mindset, meditating, exercising, avoiding bad habits, sacrificing ordinary things to make time for work hours, and—after tonight's class—engaging 5 to 20 weekly hours in high-impact activities. It's a comprehensive course of habits and work."

"Yeah, but it still sounds . . . underwhelming."

"And that's exactly the truth about success. It's underwhelming in the real world. It's not sophisticated, fun, and sexy. It's mundane, boring, and consistent. It's daily habits and hours. What else is there to success besides habits and hours?"

Sara opened her mouth but said nothing.

Jimmy chuckled. "That's all there is to winning. The real secret of success is that the process is not any one thing, but rather the sum of daily habits and useful hours. The reason it's a secret is because everyone is looking for a complex new thing, when daily execution of basics is the key to winning."

Sara looked thoughtful.

"Listen to me," Jimmy said. "We only have three weeks left in the course. They're not about to cancel the last three classes without serious provocation. We're fine. And hear me when I say this: these people you work for, they are not in your league. You're better than them. You know it, and I know it. You can do better, so don't go in there and take any shit. And don't worry about me—I'll be fine. Now let's discuss today's lesson plan."

Sara exhaled. "Fine. It's about prioritizing actions?"

"Yes, and here's the truth," Jimmy said earnestly. "You can do everything else perfectly—set clear goals, avoid vices, exercise, sacrifice ordinary comforts, and build powerful habits—but if you get your activities wrong during those precious 5 to 20 free hours each week, your dreams will slip away. What you choose to do in these hours is everything. It's the difference between success and failure in a 5-year crusade."

Sara leaned forward. "What exactly makes an activity 'right' or 'wrong'?"

"The right activity directly moves you closer to your 5-year goal. The wrong activity keeps you busy without meaningful progress. Being busy isn't enough—we must be fully engaged in the single most important task at any given moment. And that means we need to prioritize daily."

"That makes perfect sense, but how do the boys identify the single most important task each day?"

"That's the central question of the crusade," Jimmy replied. "We use a process called 'reverse engineering.' We start with the ultimate goal—saving $100,000 in five years, for example—and then break it down into annual objectives, quarterly benchmarks, weekly targets, and daily actions. This way, each day we can clearly prioritize the one most important thing."

Sara nodded slowly. "So it's about making a conscious choice, not just randomly filling time?"

"Exactly," Jimmy said. "For example, if their income is limited, the most important task might be securing extra work or overtime. But if they're already earning enough and still struggling financially, the top priority might be mastering budgeting skills to eliminate waste. Both activities matter, both are important, but choosing incorrectly can cost them their dream."

Sara exhaled thoughtfully. "So every free hour is precious, and every task chosen matters deeply."

"That sums it up. The *Power Within* is a valuable resource, but it's entirely wasted if directed toward less important tasks. The everyday decision—about which tasks get those critical impact hours—determines everything. That's why this strategy of right action is the heartbeat of the entire crusade."

He paused, meeting her eyes. "This is the single most important lesson of the course: their dreams live or die based on how effectively they use their impact hours each week."

· · ·

That evening, Jimmy stood at the front of the room as the boys filed in. This week, for once, no additional kids staggered into the classroom like stray cats looking for a home. It was a fitting analogy, he believed, since 85% of youths in prison grew up in fatherless homes. He pushed the thought aside, not ready to forgive or forget his own family abandonment.

Jimmy waited until the classroom settled. "Tonight, we're talking about the most important thing in this entire course. If you remember only one lesson from our time together, let it be this: nothing takes the place of action, which is today's lesson."

He walked in front of the room, hands clasped behind his back. "In a small valley nestled between rolling hills, there lived an elderly wise man whose final life's mission was planting trees for future generations. He dreamed of a mighty oak forest standing proudly, offering shade and shelter long after he was gone. Determined, he committed himself to a simple and consistent practice: each week, without fail, he planted exactly ten acorns carefully into the fertile earth.

"It was not much, but he was old and frail. The first year passed quietly. The wise man faithfully planted ten acorns every single week, rain or shine. By the year's end, he had planted over 500 acorns. Yet, as he walked through the field, he saw nothing—no saplings, no signs of life, just bare ground.

"The villagers watched skeptically, shaking their heads. 'You waste your time,' they said. 'An entire year, and nothing grows. Only an old fool starts something he can't finish.'

"But the wise man simply smiled and continued planting, ignoring them and minding his business. The second year began, and each week he planted his ten acorns again, each seed mindfully placed. Still, the earth showed little change. Then, midway through the second year, something remarkable happened: tiny green shoots began pushing through the soil—the seeds from the previous year finally emerging."

Jimmy walked between the aisles. "His heart filled with quiet joy. He continued his planting each week, knowing the seeds he planted today would someday sprout. The villagers noticed the sprouts but remained unimpressed. 'All that effort,' they said quietly, 'and still so little to show.'

"In the third year, the seedlings from his first year grew slowly but steadily, reaching higher each season. The second year's seeds began sprouting too. Still, the wise man continued his weekly planting of ten acorns. Three years of diligent, consistent planting—and finally, the land showed undeniable promise, though it remained modest.

"By the fourth year, the valley began to noticeably fill with young, sturdy saplings from those earliest seeds. Villagers and passersby began stopping to admire the emerging forest, recognizing the clear results of the wise man's steady effort. Yet, undistracted by admiration, he continued planting faithfully each week, minding his business, trusting the seeds to grow.

"In the fifth year, the once-barren land transformed into a

flourishing grove of young oaks. The man stopped planting and appreciated his contribution until his final days.

"After ten years, birds nested among the branches, animals sheltered beneath their shade, and villagers walked through the thriving landscape. Now, people no longer questioned his efforts—they admired his wisdom and grit. And they erected a plaque in the forest in the deceased man's honor."

Jimmy stopped and tapped his laptop. The television screen on the wall lit up with an image of two acorns. Bold text underneath the seeds read: *Impact Hours.*

IMPACT HOURS

"Every impact hour in your day is like a seed planted in soil," he began. "They grow into your future achievement—each one is sixty minutes of goal-focused effort. Week by week, they don't seem like they'll amount to much. But over years, these little hours make a difference if you do the right things."

He pointed at the screen. "Your job each week is to plant between 5 and 20 of these impact hours—not during mandatory hours like work or school, but in your own free time. These hours engaged in the right actions are the seeds of your future harvest. And so your ongoing strategy is everything."

Jamal raised his hand. "Work smarter, not harder?"

Jimmy shook his head. "No—it's both working smarter and harder on activities that directly move you toward your goal. That means 'reverse engineering' your goal. We'll begin with the end goal clearly in mind and work backward. Ask yourself:

Where should I be at four years, three years, two, and then one? By asking these questions, you'll discover an urgent priority."

Jimmy tapped his laptop, causing the following statement to appear in bold letters on the television:

If you don't have a most important task to do now, then your most important task is to figure out your most important task to do now. Work backward from your goal.

He turned to face the class. "Reverse engineer your goal. What does that even mean? Let's use your goal of saving $100,000 in five years as an example." He tapped his laptop, and a breakdown of the math appeared on the TV screen:

$100,000 ÷ 5 years = $20,000 per year
$20,000 ÷ 12 months ≈ $1,667 per month
$1,667 ÷ 4 weeks ≈ $416 per week

The boys stared at the bottom number: $416 per week.

Slugs murmured, "Holy crap. That's a lot."

"Yes, it's challenging to save $416 per week," Jimmy acknowledged. "But now we have clarity. Let's explore ways to achieve it." He tapped the laptop again, revealing strategies:

- **Save $200 weekly from your paycheck.**
- **Work a part-time job, 15-20 extra hours per week.**
- **Start a side hustle (mowing, pet-sitting, reselling).**
- **Learn a high-demand skill to boost income.**

"Imagine saving $200 from your main job. You still need $216 weekly. That's achievable with a strategic plan involving a side job or hustle. Your goal relies on 5 to 20 weekly impact hours dedicated to tasks with the highest returns—not just random busy work. Doing the right things is the essence of strategy."

Slugs sighed. "So I gotta work two jobs?"

"That's one way to look at it," Jimmy agreed. "But here's another way to look at it. An average nurse in our country works a 40-hour shift, and then another 5 to 20 overtime hours every week. That's the same exact price of a crusade. It's no more than the nurse who works 5 to 20 overtime hours."

"It looks tiring," Slugs said.

"It can be," Jimmy admitted. "But that's precisely why most people never reach their goals. They never clearly plan their high-impact activities. They're just too busy. Let's make this relevant to owning your auto repair shop in five years."

What followed was a classroom discussion, during which the class formulated milestone goals for this final achievement. In summary, the chalkboard displayed an outline of a plan:

Year 5: Own and operate your shop.
Year 4: Manage a shop, finalize your business plan.
Year 3: Gain experience, save capital.
Year 2: Get certified, build your reputation.
Year 1: Start working at a repair shop.

Jimmy asked Slugs, "First week out, what should you do?"

"Celebrate and party?" Slugs asked.

Jamal spoke up. "Looks to me like he needs to find a job at a repair shop while tracking all the small habits and hours in this 5-year crusade system."

All heads swung slowly toward Jamal.

"I'd agree with that strategy," Jimmy said. "What you do

day in and day out trumps everything. So now we see a young man working a full-time job and managing his daily habits."

Jimmy looked around the room. "Then what?"

"It's time to plant impact hours," Jamal said. "If you want a future harvest, you gotta plant the right seeds."

"Yes, and so your free time becomes critical," Jimmy said, leading another classroom discussion. Together, the boys brainstormed tasks that would engage 5 to 20 weekly hours. At the end, the chalkboard contained a list of possibilities:

Impact Hour Tasks

- **Study auto repair basics daily.**
- **Research trade schools and apprenticeships.**
- **List potential shop owners to shadow.**
- **Apply for scholarships and training.**
- **Practice hands-on repair skills from tutorials.**

Jimmy faced the group directly. "Your impact hours—filled with strategic tasks—will decide your future. Doing anything less wastes the *Power Within.* No matter how well you master the other tasks of this course, without clearly defined action goals, you drift aimlessly, planting seeds that never grow."

Mack spoke up. "All this effort for a dirty car shop?"

Slugs seemed to sag in his chair. "It does seem like a lot."

Jimmy looked sternly at Mack, anger rising toward the bully who disparaged the dreams of an aspiring entrepreneur. At the same time, he stayed calm and turned toward Slugs.

"This reverse engineering seems like a lot, but it's a one-time thing. You just figure out some milestone goals to keep you going in the right direction. The two main routines that determine your success are prioritizing your weeks and days."

Jimmy walked to the chalkboard, and wrote.

Rule #1: Prioritize High-Impact Tasks for 5 to 20 Weekly Impact Hours.

He stepped back from the board. "Like the old man planting 10 acorns every week, you too will plant seeds every week—5 to 20 impact hours. At the start of the week, you will make weekly goals for these hours: activity goals to move the needle now. It will take you less than an hour to prioritize your week."

Jimmy turned and wrote on the chalkboard.

Rule #2: The weekly planning session is always the single most important hour of your 5-year crusade.

He turned toward the class. "This one hour determines the value, impact, and quality of many other hours. You'll write goals in a weekly planner, and at the end of the week, you'll record your achievements of the week. You'll also use this planner to write down your new inspirations, ideas, and plans.

One last time, he turned to the chalkboard.

Rule #3: Every morning, you'll review the weekly planner and prioritize ONE most important one thing to achieve.

Jimmy turned and looked at Slugs. "Once you reverse engineer your goals to get milestone goals, the hard work of thinking is behind you. In the days of a crusade, you just fill your time with high-impact activities. You prioritize the vital few things that matter most to your goals—and that's all there is to it."

"Slugs seemed to straighten. "I can do that."

"I know you can," Jimmy said. "It's not that hard, but you will need a weekly planner, and then you'll need to use it."

"So you can be a grease monkey," Mack laughed.

Jimmy took a deep breath. "Okay, Mack, let's talk about your goal then. You say you want to be a millionaire. And you expect this goal within five years."

Mack smiled. "Sooner."

"Fair enough," Jimmy said. "It's easy to fantasize about a big goal, but let's reverse engineer it now. All you need to do is add a zero to the numbers of our previous example."

He sat at his laptop, added the zeroes, and a breakdown of the math appeared on the TV screen:

$1,000,000 ÷ 5 years = $200,000 per year

$200,000 ÷ 12 months ≈ $16,670 per month

$16,670 ÷ 4 weeks ≈ $4160 per week

Jimmy noticed a few students peeking at Mack, who remained stone-faced at the sight of the impossible figures.

"So now we know the weekly goals," Jimmy said. "When you get out of here, you'll need a full-time job like everyone else. You'll follow the system of a 5-year crusade, and—"

"What if I skipped all your little habits to make time for important things that really count toward a million bucks?"

The classroom was silent. Jimmy glanced at Sara, who was observing the situation with curiosity. *Was he seriously going to support the character's quest for a million dollars in five years?* She watched Jimmy rub his chin and pause to think carefully.

"If you study these numbers for saving a million dollars in five years," Jimmy said finally, "you'll see that most ways to use your time are pointless. They just don't add up. In fact, the only way to bank that kind of money in five years, starting from scratch, is to create and sell an extraordinary business."

He looked directly at Mack. "To reach your goal, you'll need to engage all your free time beyond a full-time job to create a business you can sell. Nothing else matters. That business must serve a need, and you must see yourself as a servant of the common good. You will get rich in direct proportion to how well your business serves others—and how remarkable it is."

Mack looked less sure of himself, for once.

Jimmy tapped on the laptop, displaying the *Power Within* surrounded by shackles, with "Self-Doubt" crossed out.

Self-sabotage

Self-neglect

Self-doubt

Self-delusion

Self-contempt

Power Within

"The cure for self-doubt isn't toughness—it's having a plan that is workable. Once you know what you want, and then formulate a plan, the process is simply prioritizing your weeks and days. It's staying so busy at work that you don't have time to worry about your results. You'll find that work is easier than worry. But prioritizing your days is necessary for the work."

"Do we get points for prioritizing?" Jamal asked.

Jimmy looked at Sara, who was studying Jamal with growing interest. "Yes, you get a point to prioritize your day in a 5-year crusade," Jimmy said. "It's a simple thing that takes less than a few minutes. Each morning, you'll review your weekly planner and choose the most important task for your day."

"What's the most important task?" Mack asked.

Jimmy exhaled audibly, frustrated at the question since this lesson plan was all about it. Before he could respond, however, Jamal turned toward Mack in the back row.

"If you don't know the most important thing to do every day," he said, "it means you don't have weekly goals. If you don't have weekly goals, you didn't prioritize anything for the week. And if you don't prioritize anything for the week, you're just dreaming."

Jimmy sensed a special moment of leadership in the classroom. Without adding to it, he handed out the homework.

"Next class, we'll dissect a typical day in the life of a crusader," he said, regaining his focus. "Until then, I want you to begin to prioritize the one most important thing every day."

THE CRUSADE WAY

1. Review the Crusader's Creed for 6 minutes daily.

2. Exercise for 15-30 minutes every day until you die.

3. Abstain from 2 vices for the 30-day habit fast.

4. Meditate for 5, 10, or 15 minutes once a day.

5. Schedule 5 to 20 weekly hours of extra effort.

6. Prioritize one most important thing every day.

CHAPTER 10

D *is for* Daily

*Success is the sum of small efforts repeated day in and
day out. Make small efforts, one day at a time.*

Our potential is useless without our engagement of time.
Every condition we desire, including prosperity and
wealth, requires a price to be paid—our outcomes reflect
our hours. We miss the height of our fullest potential by
not engaging the quiet parade of days.

– Lessons of the Wealthy Gardener

As Jimmy drove to the reform school, he reflected on the nature
of the lesson he was about to teach. Engaging the *Power Within*
to achieve audacious goals wasn't about complex behaviors. Instead, it involved a prosperous lifestyle of consistent small
actions. A 5-year crusade could be reduced to a structured way
of life—one that activates the *Power Within* through intentional
daily efforts and supportive daily habits.

Today, Sara and her daughter, Faith, were seated at the

conference table when Jimmy walked into the room. It was Take Your Child to Work Day, an annual event offering kids a glimpse into their parents' careers and workplaces. After brief introductions, Sara tried to explain the purpose of this elective course to Faith, but she was having trouble simplifying it for a nine-year-old.

"The course teaches goal achievement," Sara explained. "It helps students not only survive after their parole but also thrive in the real world. It's an actionable system of small efforts and habits, repeated day in and day out."

"The problem it solves," Jimmy added, "is that too many of the boys return to jail within five years. They fail because they either forget or disregard most of what they learn in the classroom. My goal in this course is to help them not only stay out of jail but also save $100,000 within the next five years."

Faith's eyes widened. "That's a lot of money!"

Sara smiled gently. "Something that really helps them get organized is a daily checklist. It keeps all their habits and action goals in front of them. It's like a to-do list of essentials."

Jimmy took this as his cue and handed Faith a printed checklist that mirrored the Crusader's Tracker app. It included six good habits, two slots for a habit fast, and spaces to track daily hours—both regular job hours and extra impact hours.

Good habits	Bad Habits
☐ Mindset	☐
☐ Meditate	☐
☐ Prioritize	**Job hours**
☐ Exercise	☐☐☐☐☐☐☐
☐ Expectize	**Impact hours**
☐ Tracking	☐☐☐☐☐☐☐

Faith studied the checklist. "This helps them save money?"

"The daily checklist helps them stay focused on little things," Jimmy said. "It's an important part of a system to achieve hard things, including money goals. I personally follow this checklist on an app that keeps score in points. When I stop doing these small things daily, I tend to lose traction."

Faith looked at him. "I thought it was just for juvenile delinquents here. Are you a juvenile delinquent?"

Jimmy nodded. "Yes, I'm a former juvenile delinquent."

Faith stared at him with wide eyes.

"Honey," Sara said, "I have a confession. I've been using the app secretly for the past several weeks to test it. This checklist is not just for juvenile delinquents. It's for anyone with goals."

Faith nodded simply as Jimmy's mouth fell open.

"It's a system of habits and effort," Sara continued. "What else is there to success besides success habits and extra effort?"

Jimmy stared at her, slowly regaining his normal sense of composure. "How about I describe a day in the life of a crusader named Craig," he said casually. "You can mark the boxes on this checklist as we navigate his day, okay?"

"Okay, let's do it!" Faith said eagerly.

Jimmy smiled. "Craig wakes up early to do a morning routine at the start of every day," he began. "Craig's a smart guy, and he has a strategy that makes it easy to wake up early."

"An alarm clock?" Faith asked.

Jimmy chuckled. "Yes, but his main tactic is going to bed early so he can wake up early. Craig gets up, pours himself a cup of coffee, sits in his favorite chair, and reviews the Crusader's Creed. It's just a six-minute recording, like a guided meditation, and he listens to it. It helps him stay focused in his busy life, and it strengthens the *Power Within."*

"What's the *Power Within?"*

"It's your full potential, honey," Sara said.

Jimmy glanced at Sara and then back at her daughter. He pointed to the first item on the checklist. "This daily recording is the work of cultivating a winning mindset," he said.

Faith checked off *Mindset.*

"After this little routine, Craig spends five to fifteen minutes meditating to set the tone for a mindful day. Craig schedules this practice early in the day to center himself since he knows being centered is key to navigating the trials of a productive day."

Faith checked off *Meditate.*

"Next, Craig opens his weekly planner and looks at his critical goals. Based on these goals, he writes down his high-impact activities for the day. Then he chooses one of those tasks as the most important ONE thing to do that day."

"What's the most important thing?" Faith asked.

"Good question," Jimmy said. "It's an activity that has a high impact on his goal—the one task that contributes the most toward saving $100,000 in five years. Since Craig is willing to sacrifice ordinary things to achieve his extraordinary goal, he prioritizes this most important task over many other things he could be doing in his free time."

Faith checked off *Prioritize.*

"Next, Craig slips into his workout clothes," Jimmy said, "because he knows starting the day with exercise is the easiest way to feel good and boost his attitude. Craig exercises for fifteen to thirty minutes to dissolve stress and restore his mind."

Faith checked off *Exercise.*

"Now that Craig is done with his morning routine, he gets ready and drives to work. Craig works four hours before lunch, focusing on one task at a time to be most effective."

Faith found *Job Hours* on the checklist and marked four boxes.

"Let's review Craig's weekday so far in this 5-year crusade," Jimmy said. "He engaged in his morning routine and worked four hours at his job. He's just doing a little bit more every morning, and nobody even sees the difference."

"Yeah, really," Faith said.

Jimmy chuckled as he saw Faith roll her eyes.

"So Craig has a lunch break. He eats with his buddies, but then he goes off to be alone for ten minutes. As he does every day, Craig uses those ten minutes to do a daily ritual that I call 'expectize.' He doesn't just visualize his goals, he expectizes his goals as done, right now, crystallizing these goals in his mind. Craig knows he usually gets in life what he expects, so he takes time every day to practice expecting great things."

Faith checked off *Expectize.*

"After lunch, Craig works for another four hours at his job," Jimmy said. "And because he focuses on one task at a time, staying centered despite interruptions and distractions, he gets his work done and finishes his day without being exhausted."

Faith placed four more checks under *Job Hours.*

"But let's not forget, Craig wants to save $100,000 in five years, and that's a lot of money," Jimmy continued. "So, after his regular job is done, he knows it's time for EXTRA efforts. What he does in these hours depends on his 5-year goals."

"So what's he do after work?" Faith asked, smiling.

Jimmy smiled back. "Let's make it interesting and say Craig wants to start an online business, something he knows nothing about. Craig's obstacle is his ignorance, so he studies for two hours after work to research and learn about online businesses.

The most important thing is educating himself. In a crusade, these hours of extra work are called 'impact hours.'"

Faith checked two boxes under *Impact Hours*.

"We just completed a full weekday in a 5-year crusade," Jimmy said. "The only thing left is to record what Craig did on the daily checklist. Can you place a check beside Tracking and tell me what Craig accomplished on his list?"

Faith checked off *Tracking*.

"Craig did a bunch of good habits," Faith said. "He worked eight hours at his job, then two more hours at night. It's a lot like me going to school all day and then doing homework in the evening. That's kinda what Craig did today."

"Exactly," Jimmy agreed. "This list can seem like a lot, but Craig is doing what most students do. And he has flexibility. He can put in the extra effort for his goals in the evenings, early mornings, or on weekends. It doesn't matter when he does the extra effort, as long as he gets it done every week. And the only way to get it done is to sacrifice a few ordinary things."

"I get that," Faith said. "My mom says that I can't have it all. She's always telling me that I gotta choose what I want most over what I want now."

Jimmy stared at her. "Can I ask you a personal question?"

Faith grinned. "Of course."

"If your mom had a secret dream, would you mind if she missed some of your activities, not all of them, to offer some extra weekly impact hours in exchange for her dream?"

"I'd be mad at her," Faith said, looking angrily at her mother, "if she didn't go after her dream, just like she always tells me to go after mine."

Jimmy glanced at Sara, who was speechless.

■　■　■

Later that evening, Sara sat quietly in the back row as Jimmy prepared at the podium. Three new boys showed up tonight, and they had to borrow desks from another room. As the classroom became quiet, Jimmy tapped a key on his laptop, and an image appeared on the TV. All eyes stared at the picture of a middle-aged pilot, smiling in uniform, standing next to a large plane.

"There was once a skilled pilot renowned for his precision, steady nerves, and unwavering confidence," Jimmy began, causing the kids to take notice. "For more than twenty years, he flew passengers safely across continents and oceans. Every day began the same way: a careful review of a simple yet vital checklist. It was methodical and predictable, but it was precisely this predictability that had ensured his remarkable safety record.

"Over the years, the pilot grew bored of the checklist. 'Why waste time repeating tasks I already know by heart?' he asked himself. Gradually, his confidence turned into complacency. One day, convinced that his experience alone was sufficient, he decided to skip the checklist entirely.

"The first few flights went without incident, reinforcing his belief. However, on a rainy afternoon, a seemingly routine flight quickly descended into chaos. A minor technical detail—one that would have been caught instantly by following the checklist—went unnoticed. As the aircraft soared above stormy clouds, alarms blared, and the plane shuddered violently. Panic filled the cabin.

"In the midst of the turmoil, the pilot felt a surge of dread. He realized, too late, that he'd allowed pride and habit to overshadow wisdom. 'How did I miss something so obvious?' he wondered desperately. Through sheer luck and his decades of experience, he managed to stabilize the plane and land safely, but the damage was done—both to the plane and to his reputation.

"On the ground, humbled and shaken, he reflected deeply on his mistake. He realized that it wasn't incompetence or lack of skill that had nearly ended in tragedy, but simply his choice to abandon the disciplined ritual of checking, step-by-step, every important detail. The checklist had never been a mere formality; it was a guardian against human frailty, forgetfulness, and overconfidence.

Jimmy paused a long and dramatic moment.

"The pilot never flew again without his checklist, no matter how routine the flight seemed. And every time he carefully reviewed each step, he silently thanked the wisdom behind the simple act of structured reminders.

"The moral became clear, etched forever in his mind: success—whether flying across an ocean or pursuing life's greatest ambitions—isn't just about skill or experience. It's about disciplined consistency in small, crucial actions each day. Just as pilots trust a checklist to safely guide every flight, we too must embrace daily habits and structured reminders to navigate our life's most ambitious journeys safely and effectively.

"This is the essence of the Crusader's life—a life of daily intentionality, supported by a reliable, ever-present checklist, ensuring we never stray too far from the habits that truly matter."

He touched a key on his laptop. The TV displayed a checklist: six daily habits, two habit-fast boxes, rows to account for job hours, and rows to mark impact hours.

"This checklist holds every action you need," Jimmy said. "Just simple, essential habits and focused hours. That's how you unlock your *Power Within*—nothing more."

Slugs muttered, "Looks like a lot of habits and hours."

Jimmy grinned. "Could you do it for one day?"

Slugs hesitated, studying the checklist. "I dunno. That's a lot for me. Discipline isn't exactly my thing."

Mack chuckled, prompting Jimmy to glance at him. "Something funny?"

"He can't handle small things."

"But you can?" Jimmy asked pointedly.

"I can easily do every habit, plus 20 impact hours," Mack said confidently, clearly lying. "I am a master crusader."

Jimmy sighed. "Well, you are impressive, Mack. Now for the rest of us, how about we break down this system into manageable chunks, starting with a simple morning routine?"

Jimmy glanced around the classroom, his eyes finally resting on Slugs. It seemed most of the boys appreciated this idea.

"Most of what you do in a 5-year crusade is a secret life that nobody will ever see. Aside from your impact hours, it looks like a normal, everyday life. Your crusade is mostly invisible."

Jimmy pointed to the screen. "Here's your morning: Review the Crusader's Creed, meditate briefly, pick your top task for impact hours, and do a short exercise routine. That's your crusade morning—simple and effective. Done in less than an hour."

He looked at the boys. "How can you do those things?"

The students looked perplexed, but Jimmy just waited in silence. After a while there were chuckles. Jimmy waited patiently.

Jamal laughed. "You just wake up and do them."

"Good answer," Jimmy said. "Now raise your hand if you can do those four things. Not for a lifetime, but just for a day. Not forever. Just for a day. Four things. One day. That's all."

Most of the students raised their hands quickly. Several of them, including Slugs, hesitated but slowly raised their hands.

"Hmmm," Jimmy said, rubbing his chin. "So you can all do it just for a day. And that's all I will ever ask you to do."

Jimmy bent over his laptop and clicked a key. The TV displayed the checklist. Four habits appeared checked off.

Good habits	Bad Habits	
☑ Mindset	☐	
☑ Meditate	☐	
☑ Prioritize	**Job hours**	
☑ Exercise	☐☐☐☐☐☐☐	
☐ Expectize	**Impact hours**	
☐ Tracking	☐☐☐☐☐☐☐	

"Next," he continued, "you expectize. That is a ten-minute guided meditation—we'll talk about it more next class. You'll focus on your goals and practice expecting them as if they are already done. Who can find ten minutes for a guided meditation? And by that I mean, who can do it for just one day?"

The boys snickered, then raised their hands.

Jimmy touched his laptop. A fifth habit box appeared checked that was displayed on the list.

"Now we'll talk about work. After your discharge, you'll work to earn a living. Raise your hand if you can work eight hours a day to avoid starvation and sleeping in the streets."

All hands slowly went up, along with a few chuckles.

Jimmy clicked his laptop. Eight job hours appeared marked on the checklist displayed on the TV screen.

"Notice that by doing a morning routine, refocusing at lunch, and working eight hours for a living, you've filled most of your day. Only habit tracking and impact hours remain. Habit tracking is simply marking this checklist and recording it. You log what you do each night. Impact hours are when you give extra effort toward your goal. Who can commit two impact hours for just *one day* after work?"

Most of the hands rose.

Jimmy noted Mack hadn't raised his hand even once.

"That's a full crusade day," Jimmy summarized. "You've done the habits, worked at a job, and logged impact hours. The secret is simply to focus on winning one day at a time."

He paused. "You will have off days, and that's normal. You catch up on weekends. But every week, no matter what, you will log 5 to 20 impact hours. Job hours help you survive. Impact hours create your progress. This is how you break the shackles of regret and excuses. This is how you free the *Power Within*."

Slugs raised a hand. "What if I miss a day?"

"Miss a day, then catch up. Miss two days, then make up for it. The goal is consistency, not perfection. You will feel self-doubt. You will feel overwhelmed. Time engagement is the cure for both. By using these hours, you prove to yourself that you can win today, and you can win tomorrow."

Jamal asked, "Do you still live like this?"

Jimmy smiled. "I used this system to earn financial freedom. Now I work part-time and spend thirty impact hours on projects I believe in. I choose this life because I know that when I give effort, I awaken my inner strength. I work in my free time."

Slugs leaned forward. "If you're free, why work at all?"

"Because work gives me a purpose," Jimmy said. "When I stopped working, I felt lost. I learned that action, not comfort, is the source of genuine happiness. The *Power Within* compels us to use our talents, and we feel empty when we don't."

Another boy asked, "So we gotta do all this for $100,000?"

"Forget the money. This is about growth. You'll become stronger, more capable, more resilient. The money is proof that you followed the process. When you use your free time for impact hours, you change your life. You change your future."

A boy pushed back. "The checklist looks impossible."

Jimmy nodded again. "It looks that way until you start. It seems that way until you focus on just one day. But four habits take one hour. The other two habits take fifteen minutes each. Eight hours at work fill your day. Then two hours of extra effort. It is the workload of many professions. You only need to win one day at a time. You only need to win this one day."

He paused, looking at Mack. "And when you cheat the system, you're only cheating yourself. This system is how you unlock the *Power Within*. Not by thinking about it. Not by waiting for motivation. By showing up—day in and day out."

The boys stared at the list on the screen.

"What if I don't want to live this way?" Slugs said.

"You don't have to live this way," Jimmy said. "But before you make a decision, why not give it a try? There will be a challenge at the end of this course to experience this way of life."

Jimmy touched a button on the laptop, displaying an image on the TV of a person who had walked on an ethereal pier over a vast ocean in darkness and was now entering the light.

"When you fully tap into your potential, it's as if you walk into a new reality. You'll be compelled, pulled, and inspired. You'll know what to do and how to avoid mistakes in advance. You'll experience coincidences and breakthroughs you can't explain. Life aligns when you're connected with your inner power, and you experience quiet ease and peace. You no longer feel hurried and impatient. You feel powerful—and you become the power."

"What's that even mean?" Mack asked.

"It means the *Power Within* is capable of causing inspiration, coincidences, and lucky breaks," Jimmy said matter-of-factly. "Next class, I'll show you how to use your power to do exactly that."

THE CRUSADE WAY

1. Review the Crusader's Creed for 6 minutes daily.
2. Exercise for 15-30 minutes every day until you die.
3. Abstain from 2 vices for the 30-day habit fast.
4. Meditate for 5, 10, or 15 minutes once a day.
5. Schedule 5 to 20 weekly hours of extra effort.
6. Prioritize one most important thing every day.

CHAPTER 11

E *is for* Expect

You get in life not what you want but
what you expect. Practice expecting more.

When I was at my best in this world, the skies opened and
rained uncanny breaks, inspirations, coincidences, and rare opportunities upon me. My good fortune was not all from my own
hands. But then again, without the work of my own hands, I
would have surely died in a drought instead of prospering. I
worked hard, but also sensed an Unseen Force working with
me, beside me, and through me.

– Lessons of the Wealthy Gardener

Jimmy and Sara walked around the circular track within the
barbed wire fences of the juvenile detention center. The day was
overcast and gloomy, and Jimmy was pensive. He reflected on
the finality of the course, Behavioral Wealthology, and why the
majority of his former students eventually engaged in criminal
activities despite all he'd taught them.

"I believe expectation is the governing force of what we get
in life, for better or worse," he said. "If we think we're stuck in

life, we're stuck. If we expect to change things, we change things. When we expect good things, we tend to get good things. When we expect bad things, we tend to get bad things. So, in this final class before the challenge, I'm going to speak about the power of expectancy."

"Yes, you plan to teach them to expect the supernatural, bend reality, and cause beneficial coincidences with the force of their minds. Is this final lesson necessary? It may affect the credibility of the course, and I'm obligated to report every nuance of your lessons to a very traditional administration."

Jimmy walked a few steps in silence.

"This lesson may affect the credibility of this class, but the power is real," he said. "I either have the courage to teach what I know is true—or I don't. As for credibility, I want to clarify that expectizing is not wishful thinking. It's a learned skill—a mindset of doubtless knowing about an outcome. It's more than praying, visualizing, attracting, or begging for favors. I couldn't find a word that did it justice, so I call it expectizing."

"You made up your own word for it?"

"Yes, and the word is *expectizing*. It's a daily practice of mentally constructing and expecting a goal. When I say constructing, I mean creating the end goal as a concrete reality in the mind."

"How exactly do you do that?"

"Here's the simple plan," Jimmy said. "Once a day, spend ten minutes knowing beyond any doubt that your goal is achieved—a done deal. You build inner vision, and you experience an inner knowing. This practice trains your subconscious to work toward its realization."

"So it's mental conditioning?"

"Yes and no. Expectizing isn't just mental conditioning; it's a practical daily method to influence the quantum field. The mental practice doesn't feel like 'ATTRACTING' goals toward me; it feels more like 'RADIATING' goals and desires outward, in a state of bold faith, as if issuing orders to the Universe. It's not an easy skill to master, but expectizing, when you do it right, feels like a sense of certainty. It then causes serendipity, lucky breaks, and coincidences. People, opportunities, and resources align with you in unexpected ways."

"So you advocate blind faith?"

"Some call it faith. Some call it physics. And some call it awareness. But I know this: when you expectize daily, reality starts bending in your favor. You'll see doors open, conversations shift, books appear, and weekly goals just get easier—not by chance but by alignment. I don't really care what students believe, or what they call it, as long as they actually try it. The skill is to build a mindset of profound trust, beyond any reasonable doubt, that what you want is already yours now."

Silence filled the space between them.

"Why are you so skeptical?" Jimmy asked.

"Because it lacks empirical evidence," Sara said. "Correlation doesn't equal causation. If you visualize and expect success and then achieve it, it's due to effort, circumstances, or luck, not just because you expected it."

"Fair enough, but why does it have to be one or the other? The practice of expectizing isn't just daydreaming. It's priming the brain to compel your actions, see opportunities, and get in the flow of inspiration. Neuroscience supports this; the mind's reticular activating system filters information and helps us notice things aligned with our focus."

"Yes, attention matters," Sara said, "but you're dressing up basic psychology in mystical language. Visualizing a goal with fierce expectancy might help focus our attention, but that doesn't mean the universe conspires to help us."

"Doesn't it, though? Look at how many successful people—

actors, athletes, entrepreneurs—credit their success to visualization or prayer. Research it online. People today openly discuss the power of expectation, often calling it manifesting. Even Steve Jobs believed in what he called 'reality distortions.' Is it possible that all these successful people are delusional and only cynics are correct in their views? Or is it more likely that skeptics are just ignorant and unaware of what they can't see?"

Sara flinched. "Ouch. I'm not saying all believers are delusional, but they're prone to confirmation bias. They see only the hits and ignore the misses. For every successful manifester, there are countless others who visualize and fail."

"True, but could that failure stem from a lack of expectancy or follow-through?" Jimmy asked. "It's not easy to generate the kind of bold expectancy that engages the quantum field and causes the Universe to take notice and conspire. How many of those failed cases actually stuck with a daily practice of expectizing for a full month, in spirit as well as in action? If someone half-heartedly expectizes, it's unlikely to work. People often stop trying before it starts working."

"Faith alone does not bend reality," Sara said. "It might help with confidence or motivation. But external factors, such as resources, networks, and skills, all play a bigger role. You're simplifying a complex process."

"Or maybe you're complicating it," Jimmy said. "We tend to get what we expect in life. When we expect good things, we tend to get good things. When we expect bad things, we tend to get bad things. Is it possible we're all subconsciously using the power of expectancy?"

"I'll give you that mindset matters," Sara agreed, "but attributing random luck to focused expectation feels like impractical nonsense. What about people in dire circumstances? Are you saying they failed because they don't believe hard enough or they expect the worst?"

"Not at all," Jimmy answered. "The mental force of expectation isn't about blame; it's about empowerment. Circumstances can be harsh, but even in tough conditions, an attitude of stubborn expectancy can lead to uncanny coincidences and a flow of serendipity."

"Or it can lead to real actions and choices that cause results."

Jimmy chuckled. "Okay, maybe I can't prove it works, but I believe it works based on too many coincidences that I can't explain. If I'm wrong, what's the harm? I increased my focus and raised my expectations. The practice of expectizing doesn't take the place of work in a crusade. Why not suspend your disbelief and try it? I'm only suggesting a thirty-day experiment."

Sara thought deeply before answering. "I think I'll pass on the offer. I'm just not blessed with the gift of faith. I need proof before I can believe."

"Fair enough," he said. "But while you're waiting for proof, I'm going to teach a 30-day experiment to explore the power of expectizing. It will be an optional class assignment. You might consider participating to gather your own proof. You have nothing to lose."

Sara chuckled. "I'm not wired for expectizing."

"Suit yourself," Jimmy said, a gleam in his eye. "Just don't be surprised if one day you realize you've been expectizing all along."

· · ·

That evening, Jimmy surveyed the classroom. He felt responsible for helping these young men who attended his elective night class at the juvenile detention center. Their voluntary attendance showed their ambition. But he knew the real test would begin next week with the start of the challenges of a crusade.

Jimmy cleared his throat and began with a parable.

"There was once an artist who lived in a small coastal village, creating paintings filled with vibrant colors and soulful expressions admired by everyone who saw them. Despite his obvious talent, he struggled to sell his art and lived on the edge of poverty. Over time, his optimism faded, replaced by empty resignation. Each day felt more mundane, each painting forced, as he slowly accepted a life of quiet disappointment.

"One afternoon, the richest man in the village, respected for his success and insight, noticed the artist's growing despair. He approached the artist and spoke plainly. 'I see your fading hopes,' he said, 'not only in your attitude but in your work. And so, I will offer you a word of advice. People think my success comes purely from hard work, but that's only partly true.

"'The deeper truth is simpler—I always expect good things to happen. And then good things happen. Maybe it's luck, maybe coincidence, or perhaps it's because when we expect good outcomes, we look for ways to create them. I can't explain exactly how it works, but faith has a power all its own.'

"He walked away. His words touched the artist profoundly. Though skeptical, the artist decided to test this unsolicited advice. Each morning, he began intentionally expecting something good to happen. He imagined people noticing and appreciating his paintings. He envisioned new opportunities and believed in possibilities he'd long dismissed as improbable.

"Initially, little seemed to change. Days passed quietly, testing his resolve. But slowly, a subtle transformation occurred within him. His renewed optimism changed how he interacted with others and how he approached his work. He presented his paintings with greater confidence, spoke more passionately about his art, and connected more deeply with those around him."

Jimmy paused dramatically as he scanned the room.

"Then something unexpected happened. Travelers and visitors started to pause longer at his paintings, drawn in by their emotional depth. Word quietly spread, and his reputation grew. Soon, a gallery owner, visiting the village by chance, was captivated by his work and commissioned several pieces for her gallery. Shortly after, a prominent art collector, deeply moved by his sincerity and passion, purchased many of his paintings and enthusiastically shared his talent with others.

"Reflecting on his journey, the artist was often amazed at how expecting better outcomes had transformed his life. Had his expectant attitude attracted good fortune, or had it simply led him to take the actions necessary to create these opportunities? He could never be certain. But one thing became clear—there was never a good reason not to practice expecting more."

Jimmy walked to the podium and stood behind it.

"In this lesson, we'll talk about uncommon powers, requiring absurd faith, and using your full concentration. But first, I want to prepare you for the discomfort you will experience if you have the courage to expect more than an ordinary life."

Jimmy touched his laptop, and the TV suddenly displayed an image from a previous lesson. It was the image of a human brain, surrounded by the words Try, Suffer, and Rise. Arrows pointed from one word to the next, forming a cycle around the brain: Try. Suffer. Rise.

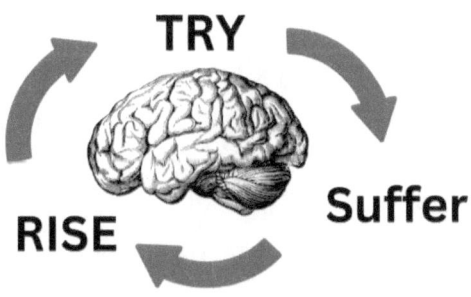

"This cycle is called The Way of the Cross," Jimmy said, "referring to the three-year ministry crusade of Jesus Christ. I don't care what your religion is; you've got to give credit where credit is due, and that was a serious crusade. It's important to see this example now and realize that in the next five years, you will also TRY, SUFFER well, and RISE to your full potential."

"How much suffering you talkin' about?" Slugs asked, causing ripples of laughter.

"It varies," Jimmy said honestly. "Raising your expectations will leave you vulnerable to disappointment. In fact, some will say that expectation is the source of all suffering. They will tell you to expect less. It may be true that expecting less is one way to avoid pain—but it is also a way to limit your *Power Within* to a safe little life that's far below your creative potential."

The class was silent. Sara in the back row watched him critically. Was he going to tell them to believe in miracles?

"I won't claim to know why expecting good results tends to lead to favorable outcomes," Jimmy said. "When you test the power of expectation and learn to master it, you are playing with a fire that engages the *Power Within* in ways that will leave you awestruck. You will see luck if you can keep the faith. Who believes that within you now is the ability to cause luck?"

Not a kid moved; not a hand was raised initially.

Jamal raised his hand. "I've witnessed it," he said. "In my business, instincts were everything. On the streets, we rely on intuition and shifts in energy that align with expectations."

Jimmy looked at him. "Explain what you mean."

"What I mean is when we expect a good outcome and get a bad feeling, something's wrong. You learn to trust it. You learn to dial in and feel your way on the streets to avoid trouble. I learned to visualize, like an athlete in a pre-game ritual."

Mack chuckled loudly. "Then how'd you get caught?"

"I got cocky, like you," Jamal said. "When you get cocky, you stop being careful. Arrogance breeds errors. You'll see."

Jimmy saw Mack stand and step menacingly toward Jamal. At the same time, four of Jamal's friends stood to face Mack.

Jimmy felt a surge of adrenaline. Losing control wasn't an option—not tonight, not ever. He moved down the aisle between them. "Sit down—all of you! And I don't mean later. Sit down this second!"

He watched them all sit simultaneously. In the corner, Sara, who was poised to intervene, relaxed slightly as Jimmy firmly handled the crisis. He commanded order with his will.

"Let's get back to work. Where were we?" Jimmy said, trying to recall his lesson plan. He looked around the room.

"You were explaining the power of expectation," Sara said from the back row. Jimmy, instantly shocked by her active help in the classroom, maintained his steady composure.

"I will teach you to command outcomes through your will," Jimmy continued. "I will now teach you how great you are, and how much greater you can be by learning to use your mind."

He found his laptop, tapped a key, and the TV displayed an image of the *Power Within*, surrounded by five inner shackles. There was an X over the shackle of Self-Contempt.

Self-sabotage

Self-neglect

Self-doubt

Self-delusion

Self-contempt

Power Within

"The hard way to achieve anything worthwhile is to pursue it with an attitude of uncertainty and self-contempt," Jimmy said. "The easy way is to know that you are more than enough. In fact, you're so worthy that even the Universe is on your side."

Jimmy noted the deep silence and allowed it.

"What's self-contempt mean?" Slugs asked.

"It means you believe you are unworthy. Like the artist in the shop, struggling every day, you don't know how great you are, or what you can do, if only you adopt a mindset of faith."

His voice was so full of conviction that a deeper silence permeated the classroom when he paused. All eyes were glued to him, and even Sara was listening more intently.

"Now let's discuss the practical aspects of expectancy," he said, transitioning to the lesson plan. "Some of you might believe in God, a Higher Power, Universal Intelligence, or simply the strength that comes from within. Whatever you believe, know that you have the ability to connect with something bigger than your current situation. You have the power to create lucky breaks, if only you focus intently on your goals, maintain a sense of inner knowing, and expectize your goals as a daily practice."

The kids looked at each other with confused expressions.

"Yes, I said 'expectize,' and I'm going to teach you how to expectize your goals. I'll walk you through a guided meditation designed to help you wrap your goals in a blanket of expectation," Jimmy explained. "We'll call it expectizing goals because it's fiercer than visualizing goals. It's entering a mental state of positive arrogance, the certainty that what you want is already yours."

The room was silent as Jimmy began to stroll.

"Just as expectizing is more than visualization, it's more than gratitude. Think of expectizing as a ritual of giving your goals a hot bath of doubtless certainty every day, knowing that you're not alone in making it happen. Your job is to build an inner knowing."

Mack groaned. "We're supposed to expect miracles?"

"You don't have to believe everything I say right now. Just try it. You're not begging, you're expecting. Open your mind a little, and see how it feels to expectize a future that's brighter than where you are today. Before we dive into it, let me give you a few caveats.

"First, it's okay if you don't believe what I claim about your full mind force. I'm not an evangelist. If you don't want to try the experiment, then don't. If you follow all the other steps of a 5-year crusade but skip this last step, you'll still be doing quite a bit to reach your goals.

"Second, this daily practice is called 'attracting' or 'manifesting' by some people, while others use the exact same technique as a 'thought experiment' to stimulate their creative imagination. Whether you want to bend reality, cause a reality distortion, or stimulate your imagination, the process is the same as the guided meditation I'll teach you today. On the daily checklist of habits, we'll refer to it as 'expectize,' but you can call it whatever you like.

"Third, be wary of your impatience," Jimmy continued. "Your confidence will grow with practice and evidence. Keep expectizing even when nothing seems to happen. Stay the course for thirty days. Live by FAITH, not by SIGHT."

"Lastly, there is no perfect way to do what I'm about to show you. In fact, my own method is imperfect. My goal is to get you started using prompts, and then you can tweak the process in your own way for best results. Don't question whether you're doing it right. Just keep doing it."

"Doing what already?" Mack grumbled.

"Engaging the *Power Within*," Jimmy said. "Today, we'll discuss how to radiate your power and become one with the Energy that grows acorns into oak trees. What we'll be doing is based on the words of the ultimate crusader from 2,000 years ago: 'Whatsoever you ask for in prayer, believe that you have received it, and it will be yours.' I don't know about the rest of you, but I'd rather listen to that man than an everyday cynic with zero experience in expectizing."

The room was still, and the kids were silent.

"So let's get started," Jimmy said. "I'll show you my personal guided meditation now with 20 second pauses between prompts. Your job is to concentrate on your goals in a state of calm expectancy, even arrogance. Pretend you're radiating your goals, issuing orders to a willing Universe. As you listen, stay in the presence of your Power Within."

Jimmy put his cell phone on speaker mode, touched the play button, and leaned back against the desk.

The Expectancy Experiment

Close your eyes. Be still. Feel My presence. I am here. I am the Power Within—the Something More in you. I have always been here. Breathe in deeply, and as you exhale, release every trace of doubt. What you seek is already yours. I have given it to you. Now, receive it.

See yourself as I see you—strong, disciplined, and unstoppable. You are already the one who has achieved your dream. See your wishes fulfilled. . . . Feel it now.

You are standing in the achievement of everything you worked for. Step into it now. You are that person now who is achieving all that, then.

Trust that I will show you the way. I am always speaking to you. Listen. The next step is already within you. Let your mind rest in calm expectancy. As you focus on your highest aspirations, know that I will always reveal what is most important to do next. Be still, and know that the path ahead is clear. It's paved now. Trust that.

Your 5-year goal is done. See it now in absolute certainty, no doubt. Allow it to be real. It is yours. Spend time with it now— see it clearly with expectation . . . imagine the pride you feel . . . the sense of accomplishment. You are sure, you are fulfilled, you are satisfied. Experience now and expect your goal achieved as a present fact.

Allow the right people to find you. I am sending the right people into your life—mentors, friends, and allies who believe in you, but who also challenge you. Open your

heart to them, and see these good people surrounding you. Feel gratitude now for them in your life. Love them. Expect them to show up at just the right time.

I make the way where there is no way. I have placed opportunities before you. They are waiting for you to step forward. See the doors open—new jobs, creative ideas, breakthroughs, unexpected turns, coincidences, lucky breaks. Walk boldly, knowing that every door I open leads to your expansion, your purpose, your highest good. Suspend all disbelief today. Walk boldly.

Stand in your power now. I made you stronger than any vice, any addiction, or any self-sabotaging tendency. Your will is aligned with mine. You choose only what uplifts you. You are free, whole, and complete. See yourself five years from now fulfilled, powerful, at peace. Your mind is sharp, your body is strong, your spirit is calm, your joy is complete. Be there and that now.

I have created you to grow, to rise, to stretch beyond your comfort. Trust the process. Be yourself, and do your best. Live one day at a time. Step into the unknown without hesitation. I have designed challenges to make you stronger. See yourself embracing stress and discomfort, knowing that you are improving, always expanding.

Know that your life will be a blessing to others. You are chosen to be a light in the dark. Your success leads others to hope. You are proving what is possible. Your story will one day inspire others with dreams of their own. See the ripple effect of your success. Be a light and lead them by your example. Show them that dreams come true.

Everything you have lived has prepared you for this moment. Nothing was wasted. Every struggle ... shaped you. Every past hardship ...strengthened you. Every mistake ... made you wiser. Look back with gratitude. Your past was never a mistake. It was my design. Now step forward, knowing I have made all things work together for your good. Look forward from now on.

Accept now that you are chosen. You are not ordinary. You were made for more. You are not waiting to be worthy—you are already worthy. The dream in your heart is already yours. I have placed it in your hands. See it. Feel it. Expect it. Command it and demand it. It is real. It is here. It is done. Practice fierce expectancy of it now.

Now, breathe. Let My words settle deep within you. Rest in this knowing. Feel gratitude rising in your heart. Smile, for it is all already yours. Write down today the coincidences that show up, according to your clarity and expectancy. As you believe, so shall it be. Carry this state of expectancy with you throughout every hour of this day. Live by faith, not by sight, and trust that you are not alone. I am with you always.

Jimmy finished and looked around the class before continuing. "If your goals aren't monetary, modify this meditation using your personal dream instead of the $100,000 emergency fund. Then use this guided meditation to build expectancy. Every day, perform this 10-minute ritual to cultivate an inner knowing. Take a daily bath in ABSOLUTE FAITH."

"Do all successful people do this crap?" Mack asked.

"You'd be surprised who meditates on outcomes and seeks inner guidance," Jimmy replied. "Search online, and you'll find many impressive people who credit their rare success to manifesting or the power of prayer. Don't let outward appearances fool you, either. Some of the most successful people have the richest inner lives, even if they don't wear it on their sleeves. A better question is, why would you NOT try expectizing for 30 days? What do you have to lose?"

The question produced a moment of silence.

"And you think we can cause lucky breaks?" Slugs asked.

Jimmy smiled. "Yes, I think it's possible to bend reality and encourage luck to flow toward you. You can enter a river of co-operative energy. The key is to foster a stubborn attitude of bold expectation in your meditation practice, and then throughout your life. It's not enough to expectize for 10 minutes and then spend your day in fear, doubt, and worry. You can achieve anything you deeply know is possible. Practice this guided meditation every day to center yourself on your 5-year goal. Then live by faith, not by sight, throughout your day. If you master expectancy, you'll begin noticing serendipity and synchronicity helping you in ways that otherwise wouldn't happen."

"What kind of ways?" Slugs asked, skeptical but curious.

With a single sheet of paper in hand, Jimmy walked to the center of the room. "To answer that question, let's review a note from a man who is no longer in this physical world. Here's what he wrote about serendipity, synchronicity, and the invisible hand of fate."

> *I am the Silent Power. I speak to you through thought flashes, hunches, inspirations, ideas, compulsions, inclinations, vibrations, and instincts. I am the sixth sense—the repulsion when something isn't quite right, the calmness when it is. I am your inner wisdom, waiting for you to pause and feel me. I am the silence of every day, seeking to guide you.*
>
> *I am the Unseen Force. I am the coincidence, the lucky break, the chance occurrence that shows up according to your abiding trust. I am the wonder, the marvel, the awe, the life, and the miracle. I am the cooperative energy, and I aid every aspiration according to your daily clarity, strategy, devotion, attention, and*

faith. I am the Something More you sense. You honor me most by struggling well in the garden.

Jimmy looked up. "The man who wrote this message was like a father and mentor to me. He was a master gardener, and the garden was his metaphor for life. It took me a while to understand that this final message was exactly where he wanted me to begin. He asked me to teach this class, and so I've done my best to introduce you to the mysterious Something More within you. You don't need to be more than you already are to win in life. You only need to free your *Power Within*."

With that, he dismissed the class and handed out the homework assignment. He instructed the boys to prepare for next week's challenge: achieving a winning score for four weeks in order to master the simple lifestyle of a 5-year crusade.

THE CRUSADE WAY

1. Review the Crusader's Creed for 6 minutes daily.
2. Meditate for 5, 10, or 15 minutes once a day.
3. Exercise for 15-30 minutes every day until you die.
4. Abstain from 2 vices for the 30-day habit fast.
5. Schedule 5 to 20 weekly hours of extra effort.
6. Prioritize one most important thing every day.
7. Practice expecting more in a guided meditation

CHAPTER 12

S *is for* System

You don't rise to the level of your goals, you fall to
the level of your system. Follow a tracking system.

We track our impact statistics to focus our exertions, and to
separate everyday hustle from the key hustle that wins the
game. If we rely on memory alone, we're all superheroes of
effort. But if we keep track of impact statistics, we will often
see a truer reality of our effort.

— Lessons of the Wealthy Gardener

Sara and Jimmy sat in the lounge beside the cafeteria, the distant hum of kitchen noise filling the silence between them. A calculator sat on the table alongside the Crusader's Tracker app open on Sara's phone.

"Let me make sure I understand," Sara began. "You've created a scoring system to gamify daily actions. Each habit, job hour, and extra effort earns points, and the weekly total becomes the challenge you'll present to the boys—the weekly Crusade."

"Exactly," Jimmy replied. "You either reach the score or you don't. No excuses, no rationalizations—just clear, measurable results."

Sara nodded thoughtfully. "And the ultimate objective is to perform consistent small actions, day in and day out. Right?"

"Yes, small actions that add up to winning weeks. Four winning weeks in a row completes a level. If you miss your target of weekly points, you start over at week one."

She glanced at the app, slightly amused. "Well, I've been quietly keeping track myself for the past few weeks. Honestly, it's both motivating and humbling."

Jimmy smiled. "What's your average score?"

Sara sighed softly. "Usually around 70 to 75 points a week. I work full-time, consistently track my habits, and exercise regularly—but I haven't put in much beyond the basics."

"So that's your baseline," Jimmy explained. "Think of this as your starting point—you're responsible and consistent, but not yet pushing into Crusader territory."

"So to become Crusader Sara," she said, smiling faintly, "I need to level up."

"Right," Jimmy agreed. "The first official Crusader level is 99 to 110 points. It's about stretching beyond the routine of an ordinary lifestyle. That means consistent daily habits, resisting negative habits, plus job hours."

"I'm already doing that."

Jimmy smiled knowingly "So what's the solution?"

Sara studied the points on tracker app, then finally looked up. "Do more habits, and do them more consistently."

"The system is the solution," Jimmy said. "If you want more achievement, earn more points. If you want more points, do more in the system. The system makes you focus on the process."

Sara smiled impressively. "I noticed exercise and tracking earn more points than the other habits. Why is that again?"

"Exercise takes extra discipline," Jimmy said. "And tracking is the backbone—it maintains your awareness. Lose that, and the system collapses. Without tracking, you lose everything."

"Makes sense," Sara replied. "What about weeks when things don't go perfectly?"

"The system is forgiving," Jimmy assured her. "You're scoring weekly, not daily. If one day slips, you can still compensate another day. A crusader focuses on total weekly points, not daily perfection."

Sara looked down at her current score—64 points with two days remaining. It was possible to reach a crusade level score, but she'd need to focus each day to hit the first-point range.

"And what happens after completing four winning weeks?"

"You either maintain your current level or level up by adding impact hours," Jimmy said. "Regular job hours earn one point each, but impact hours—the extra work toward meaningful goals in your free time—earn three points each. They're voluntary, intentional, and transformative."

Sara sighed, letting her guard down for once. "And that's exactly what I've been missing—those extra, intentional hours dedicated to growth. I used to study more hours than I worked at my job when I was getting my degrees. I graduated and…"

"And then you stopped," Jimmy said. "We all do it. We graduate from high school or college, and we stop working in our free time. I have a theory about why that's so universal."

"Please do tell."

"It's because academia lays out a clear structure. We know what we need to do, and we either do it or we fail. It's not so clear when we're out of school. Success requires more of an entrepreneurial mindset. We need to do things without anyone watching, without deadlines, and without even the certainty of satisfying progress. Worse, we see no real punishment for procrastination. We have the luxury of drifting without pain."

"Are you suggesting these are my issues?"

"No, but I think you avoid uncertainty," Jimmy said. "It's why you choose to stay in a job you dislike rather than walk into the discomfort of the unknown. You fear uncertainty so much that you limit your possibilities. That's not freedom."

Sara remained calm. Her initial rush of defensiveness dissolved into acknowledgment, then turned into shame. When exactly had she started coasting? How had comfort silently turned into complacency? God only knew he was right.

She finally sighed. "Okay, but how about you? After all the inner work of a crusade—defeating these five inner demons, the shackles of a five-headed monster—you must be free, right?"

Jimmy shrugged. "Yeah, I am free."

"But still," Sara said, eyeing him critically, "you always have a need to prove yourself. Why? On top of that, you refuse contact with your family… that doesn't sound too free to me."

Jimmy stopped breathing. He felt his chest tighten, the sting of her words hitting something deep and unspoken inside him. He hadn't expected her to see through him so clearly. When he finally caught his breath, he simply uttered, "I'm not perfect, Sara. I never claimed to be. It's a deep wound."

"As long as you're free," Sara said gently. "Sorry if I overstepped. I think you've done a great thing with this course. I'm going to start applying myself in this crusade. It's time I stopped settling and started living up to what I can truly achieve."

Jimmy grinned warmly. "Then welcome, officially, to your Crusade." They parted, but her words lingered with him.

. . .

Later that night, Jimmy stood quietly at the front of the classroom, his heart beating steadily with quiet conviction. As the boys settled into their seats, he knew tonight was more than a lesson; it was a turning point, a chance for each of them to see their future clearly. He took a deep breath, looked directly into their eyes, and began with a story.

"There once was a young apprentice who wished to become a master archer. Every day, under the guidance of his skilled mentor, he practiced his stance, drew the bow, and released arrows toward distant targets. Despite his earnest efforts, he rarely hit the bullseye and grew increasingly frustrated and disheartened. He practiced on his own, always facing his failure.

"One day, noticing his student's mounting discouragement, the mentor proposed a new approach. 'Today, let's make your practice into a game,' he suggested gently. He placed painted circles on the target, assigning points to each ring—more points for hits closer to the center. He explained simply, 'Every shot now has a value. Your goal isn't perfection; it's consistency and improvement. Aim to surpass your score each day.'

"The apprentice felt a spark of enthusiasm. Now, instead of seeing each missed bullseye as failure, he saw each arrow as an opportunity to gain points. Each practice session became a personal challenge to beat his previous day's score. Gradually, his focus shifted away from frustration and toward measurable, incremental progress.

"Weeks turned into months, and each day, the apprentice eagerly anticipated the chance to improve his score. His confidence grew as he tracked his progress, clearly seeing how small daily improvements accumulated into meaningful gains. What had once felt tedious now brought him excitement and joy.

"One morning, after all this persistent daily effort, the apprentice confidently drew his bow and released his arrow, watching it soar repeatedly into the bullseye. Overwhelmed by achievement, he turned to his mentor in astonishment.

"His mentor smiled knowingly. 'You see, skill isn't built overnight,' he explained. 'It grows steadily, nurtured by consistency and driven by the joy of progress. When you turned your practice into a game, you shifted your focus from perfection to improvement. And that made all the difference.'"

Jimmy walked to the center of the room, letting the story settle in silence. "This is why we will now gamify your crusade—because life is not about achieving perfection in one swift motion but rather embracing the daily challenge of incremental progress. Gamifying our efforts in a system of goal achievement ensures we remain committed, focused, and inspired, bringing out the very best of our abilities along the journey."

"It's game time, baby," Jamal said.

Jimmy heard a groan coming from Slugs as he strolled to the chalkboard. Before writing on it, he explained that the game rewards small efforts repeated day in and day out. Like the archer, each day would be about progress, not perfection. He told them they'd use a physical scorecard to track their progress.

With that initial explanation, he wrote:

Step 1: Understand the Game

Jimmy spoke clearly and directly. "The challenge of a crusade involves carefully planning your week, setting clear daily priorities, and then tracking your actions."

"Sunday night planning session," Jamal said. "If we don't

know what to do every day, we didn't set our weekly goals."

Jimmy nodded. "Each week begins by identifying the most important tasks that align with your goals. Then, every morning, you'll review those tasks to make sure both your work hours and your free hours are intentionally spent on the right activities."

Jamal banged his table. "Prioritize high-impact tasks."

Jimmy grinned, turned to the chalkboard, and wrote:

- **Habits:** Good daily habits minus bad habits.
- **Hours:** Your regular job hours plus impact hours.

He turned, his tone steady. "To earn points in a crusade, you'll consistently track two key things—your daily habits and your hours. This isn't complicated, but it requires daily attention. Your habits and hours add up, creating a clear picture of how effectively you're working toward your goal each week."

"You are what you do," Jamal said.

"And when you track what you do," Jimmy added, "there's no place to hide. The weekly score exposes your real effort, just like a scale exposes your real weight. It can be uncomfortable."

He paused. "Your habits and hours add up to a weekly point total that measures your self-empowerment and self-engagement—the two foundational pillars of a 5-year crusade."

Jamal raised his hand. "How do we earn points?"

"Glad you asked," Jimmy said, writing on the chalkboard.

Step 2: Learn the Point System

"In the weekly crusade challenge," Jimmy said, "you'll use a checklist that turns habits and hours into points. Each good habit you complete earns points: mindset, meditation, prioritizing, and expectizing each earn one point daily. Two key habits—exercise and tracking your progress—are worth three points each due to their crucial impact on your progress."

"A workout reboots the mind," Jamal said.

Jimmy nodded. "And it restores the *Power Within*." He tapped his laptop, displaying a scorecard on the TV screen. It looked like a checklist with points beside each item.

Good habits		Habit fast (-1)
☐ Mindset	(+1)	☐
☐ Meditate	(+1)	☐
☐ Prioritize	(+1)	**Job hours** (+1)
☐ Exercise	(+3)	☐☐☐☐☐☐☐
☐ Expectize	(+1)	**Impact hours** (+3)
☐ Tracking	(+3)	☐☐☐☐☐☐☐

Jimmy pointed to the section on the scorecard labeled Habit Fasting. "In a crusade, you're committing to break bad habits in a 30-day habit fast—two bad habits at a time. Every bad habit you slip into subtracts one point from your daily score."

"We're penalized for bad habits?" Slugs asked.

"As in the real world," Jimmy said, "so too in the game. You get penalized for bad habits as negative reinforcement."

Jamal smiled. "Bad habits dull your brain, Slugs."

Slugs tried to protest, but Jimmy spoke quickly. "Let's talk about points earned in the game from your work hours. Your regular job hours earn one point per hour, reflecting your basic daily responsibilities. But here's where it gets interesting: each impact hour—those extra hours you spend intentionally working toward your goal—earns three points. That's because impact hours represent the extra effort that accelerates your progress toward your goal. It's *extra*-ordinary work."

"It's planting seeds," Jamal said, "for the harvest."

Jimmy grinned, looking at Sara. "It's planting seeds. And you don't have to plant seeds every single day. The goal is to consistently accumulate points throughout the week. A few off days won't ruin your overall weekly progress, as long as you keep your momentum and earn more points on the weekend."

Jimmy returned to the chalkboard and wrote:

Step 3: Weekly Crusade Goal

"Every item on your daily checklist has a point value," Jimmy explained. "Each day, the tasks you complete add points toward your total weekly score. The goal, then, is to achieve a weekly crusade target, like a runner aiming for weekly miles."

"A weekly point goal seems stressful," Slugs said.

"It doesn't need to be," Jimmy answered. "Let's say you want to start with a goal to work a job and master a few good habits. That's fine. You figure out the weekly points for that level of performance. That becomes your weekly crusade point goal."

"Why not just keep score without a goal?"

"Because you want to stretch yourself," Jamal said.

"I want to stretch myself on a couch," Slugs said, causing ripples of laughter. Jimmy waited for the levity to die down.

"A weekly goal motivates you in the game," Jimmy continued. "It's like the archer who tracked his daily performance. At first, he was frustrated, randomly shooting arrows and rarely hitting his target. But when he started keeping score daily, each practice became meaningful—he aimed for consistent improvement rather than immediate perfection. The daily scores provided clear feedback, and soon he naturally began focusing on gradually improving these measurable results."

Jimmy paused, letting the metaphor resonate. "Your weekly point goal is exactly the same. It's objective feedback showing you how well you're sticking to your plan and where you can improve. You don't need perfect days; you need consistent progress. Each weekly total clearly shows your progress, keeping your attention on measurable improvement, just like the archer."

Jamal smiled. "Just win one day at a time."

Jimmy noticed many students nodding thoughtfully, the metaphor of the archer clearly connecting with them. He tapped his laptop, displaying the first crusade level and its weekly point goal on the TV screen.

Crusade Level One
Goal: 99–110 Weekly Points

"This is your first challenge," Jimmy said. "You will work a full-time job or, in your case, be a full-time student, and focus on building self-empowerment habits. You'll also focus on eliminating two vices or bad habits that are weighing you down. That's all there is to Level One. You win this challenge by earning 99 to 110 points in a week. It's the baseline and easiest level. You do things to build the *Power Within*."

"It's gettin' your shit together," Jamal wisecracked.

"It's definitely that," Jimmy agreed.

"Where are the impact hours?" Slugs asked.

"In the next challenges," Jimmy said.

He touched his laptop, and the TV changed to a new screen.

Crusade Level Two
Goal: 112–125 Weekly Points

"To win the next level," Jimmy said, "you'll start giving extra effort in your free time, measured and tracked as impact hours. You'll need at least 5 weekly impact hours to meet the point challenge at this level. In practical terms, you'll have a full-time job, master daily habits, and log five weekly impact hours. Your weekly crusade point goal to achieve this second challenge is between 112 and 125 points."

"We sacrifice ordinary things," Jamal said, "to make time to do what matters most for extraordinary goals."

Jimmy waited for questions, then tapped his laptop, causing the TV screen to display the next challenge level:

Crusade Level Three
Goal: 126–140 Weekly Points

"If you choose to level up, you move on to Level Three—and let's not make this weekly challenge too complicated," Jimmy said. "To reach Level Three, you add five more weekly impact hours. That is, you'll have a full-time job, master daily habits, and clock 10 total impact hours. Your weekly point goal to achieve this third challenge is between 126 and 140 points. Any questions so far?"

"It's just ten overtime hours?" Slugs asked.

"Ten hours in the evenings, mornings, or weekends," Jamal said. "It's just a regular job plus some overtime."

Jimmy looked at Sara, who was watching Jamal with growing appreciation of the student who had taken to the course.

Crusade Level Four
Goal: 141–170 Weekly Points

"This final challenge requires more effort," Jimmy said. "Some people say they give more than 20 extra hours every week to reach their goals, and maybe it's true—but most of them don't track what they do, so it's usually an exaggeration."

"They're livin' in self-delusion," Jamal said.

"People don't mean to exaggerate," Jimmy said. "We just don't know what we actually do unless we track. I used to think I worked out almost every day. When I started tracking, I realized I exercised about four days a week. Tracking makes it real, and you'll see that 20 impact hours takes genuine planning and clear boundaries. It can be challenging."

"We're back to weekly planning," Jamal said.

Jimmy thought for a moment. "You'll definitely need to set weekly goals and plan daily tasks to reach 20 impact hours each week. You'll need to say no—often. To win the Level Four challenge, you'll maintain a full-time job, master daily habits, and log 20 weekly impact hours. Your weekly point goal for this challenge is between 141 and 170 points."

Jimmy walked to the center of the room. "Any questions?"

Jamal raised a hand. "So what's the end game?"

"You win a week by earning the required points for that level. You win a level by achieving the weekly point goal for four consecutive weeks. After you win four weeks in a row, you can level up to the next challenge. If you miss your weekly goal, you simply start again at Week One and aim once more for four consecutive winning weeks."

"So then what?" Slugs asked.

"Once you've mastered four consecutive weeks, you'll have experienced the way of a crusade. Most people think they know something because they study it, but certain things need to be lived. You need to experience the crusade life consistently to truly understand this simple way of achieving big goals."

"What do we do after four good weeks?" another student asked.

"You can level up to the next challenge," Jimmy said. "Or repeat the current challenge. Or level down to continue at a more sustainable pace."

"So it's a game without an end?" Mack scoffed loudly. "You created a fucking game with no end? You gotta be kidding me!"

Jimmy glared for a long moment. "I warned you that we speak respectfully in this class," he said evenly.

"What can you do about it?" Mack cackled. "Kick me out of the last lesson in the final minutes of the class?"

Jimmy walked slowly down the aisle. "You chose this yourself, Mack. I warned you twice. This is strike three—you're out."

Jimmy motioned toward the door.

Mack stood defiantly, clearly not intending to leave. Sara swallowed hard, her pulse quickening. She braced herself, certain she was about to witness a violent altercation.

Off to the side, Jamal stood slowly. Then Slugs stood as well. One by one, every student in the class rose, facing the bully in the back row. Mack's eyes darted nervously around the room.

"You can leave now," Jimmy said coldly.

Mack flipped his desk with one hand and stormed out of the room. The boys sat down; Jimmy returned to the front of the room. A sense of solidarity now filled the classroom.

"He's wrong about there being no end," Jimmy said. "Every 5-year crusade is a temporary journey to advance a cause. The sacrifice comes to an end, but the achievement remains. Focus on the process, and the goal takes care of itself. You'll earn your reward—and also the pride and satisfaction that comes with it."

Jimmy thoughtfully surveyed the classroom.

"And then we'll start over," Jamal said. "We'll set bigger goals based on where we are after the next five years."

Jimmy nodded. "Exactly. After every five years, you'll be a new person in a new place, with a deeper understanding of this thing we call life. It's best not to imagine what you'll want in five years—just focus on this week. Your future will take care of itself."

Jimmy passed out the homework. "And never forget one thing: you don't need to be more than you are. You only need to free the *Power Within* that you already possess. Just be yourself."

THE CRUSADE WAY

1. Review the Crusader's Creed for 6 minutes daily.
2. Meditate for 5, 10, or 15 minutes once a day.
3. Exercise for 15-30 minutes every day until you die.
4. Abstain from 2 vices for the 30-day habit fast.
5. Schedule 5 to 20 weekly hours of extra effort.
6. Prioritize the most important thing every day.
7. Practice expecting more in a guided meditation.
8. Set a weekly crusade point goal to achieve.
9. Achieve four winning weeks in a row.
10. Continue, level up, or level down for 5 years.

CHAPTER 13

Closure

Few of us can accept the pain of saying "no" to our dreams, and so we cleverly deceive ourselves with the thought of going for it someday. Someday is an excuse to avoid the immediate discomfort and anxiety of change. Someday leads to a passive inaction, and the regrets of abandoning our dreams are not immediate.

— Lessons of the Wealthy Gardener

Jimmy sat alone in his car, facing the small house he hadn't seen since he was sixteen. Twilight softened its edges but not the ache it stirred within him. For years, he'd stood in front of classrooms, speaking confidently about freedom and living in alignment with the *Power Within*. He'd urged his students to face their hardest truths head-on.

Yet here he was, thirty-one years old, sitting motionless—gripped by discomfort, uncertainty, and even a little fear.

A familiar voice in his mind whispered clearly, *This is it, Jimmy. If you don't face this, all your lessons mean nothing.*

He clenched the steering wheel, heart pounding, remembering the trial, the silence from the bench behind him. Not one

word. Not one glance. Just emptiness as his parents disappeared, leaving him to be escorted away in handcuffs to a
juvenile detention center. Resentment hardened inside him,
carrying him safely through prison and beyond—but at what
cost? He'd found a mentor, achieved wealth, developed a
course, but all of his success hadn't healed the wound.

He'd spent fifteen years nurturing bitterness like armor,
never noticing how it restricted his own heart.

You tell them to follow their Power Within. The voice grew
louder now, fierce and uncompromising. *You teach them that
freedom comes from facing what's most uncomfortable, even painful.
You preach about honor and walking into discomfort.* Wasn't it hypocritical to advocate principles that he didn't embody himself?

Jimmy stared at the closed front door, his breath shallow,
body trembling. He knew the truth: this wasn't about them
apologizing or welcoming him back. It wasn't even about forgiveness yet. It was about obedience—finally surrendering to
the sacred command he had preached but never fully em-
braced.

This was his crucible, the ultimate act of courage, the single
step that would make him worthy of every lesson he'd ever
taught.

Jimmy opened the car door and stepped onto the gravel
driveway, feeling the familiar presence of the *Power Within*—
compelling him. He heard the gravel crunch under his foot.

"I don't know if I can forgive them," he whispered, "but I
have to at least face them—or I'll never be completely free."

■　■　■

Sara paused outside the boardroom door, a knot tightening in her chest. What was it about this job that made her feel so small and insecure? Why did today's final meeting feel like a heart-pounding, climactic event? The men inside this room would surely listen faintly with boredom and half-interest.

She'd faced greater challenges—far harder than confronting indifferent administrators. She'd been a single mother at twenty-two, balancing a full-time job while earning two master's degrees. Determination had defined her twenties, driven by sacrifice, relentless effort, and sleepless nights.

But what had she done after earning that final degree?

Nothing. She'd stopped sacrificing her free time, stopped pushing herself forward. Instead, she'd slipped comfortably into the predictable rhythm of administrative chores, endless paperwork, and safe routines. After years of bold academic strides, she'd stalled—frozen in place, quietly obedient, afraid to risk the financial security that a stable job provided.

Why?

She knew why. Because real life was uncertain. Degrees had clear requirements; she could measure progress and control outcomes. But genuine growth—real progress in the real world—meant risk. It meant the discomfort of walking into the unknown. It meant trusting something invisible inside.

She'd always chased clearly defined goals. But the life she truly wanted—the life the *Power Within* called her toward—required something far scarier: trust in herself, trust in uncertainty.

Faith's voice suddenly cut through her memory: *"I'd be mad if you didn't go after your dream—just like you always tell me to go after mine."*

Sara swallowed hard. Her daughter—only in fourth grade—saw right through her hypocrisy. What kind of example had she become? A mother teaching bravery yet modeling fear.

She closed her eyes. Her heartbeat quickened, anger and

determination mingling fiercely inside her chest. She'd spent too many years obedient to these indifferent men behind closed doors. Too many years silencing the powerful voice within herself—the voice that now whispered clearly.

The *Power Within* had become real through Jimmy's teachings, through small daily efforts that awakened her dormant strength. The voice whispered firmly: *There is more to this life. You are more.*

Sara squared her shoulders, opened the door, and stepped forward to obey it.

■   ■   ■

Jimmy's steps crunched against the gravel as he walked slowly toward the front porch. The house hadn't changed much since his childhood—simple, worn, modest, with fading paint. An old porch swing hung from rusted chains attached to the awning.

He hesitated only briefly at the door before knocking twice, sharply, almost urgently, wanting to get this over with quickly.

A dog barked inside—an unfamiliar bark, higher-pitched than the old Lab he'd grown up with. Footsteps approached rapidly, and Jimmy felt his heart lurch into his throat. The door opened, and suddenly his mother stood there, eyes wide, lips parted, frozen in shock.

"Oh my God," she whispered, her voice trembling. Her eyes instantly welled with tears, one hand rising instinctively to her chest. "Jimmy? Is it really you?"

He swallowed, suddenly unsure of his voice. "Hey, Mom," he finally managed, softer than he intended. A small dog—a scruffy terrier—circled excitedly around his mother's feet.

She stepped forward, reaching for him but stopping

abruptly, unsure. Jimmy stood rigid, holding back, feeling every inch of the distance he'd placed between them over the years.

They stood in silence until Jimmy broke it awkwardly. "What happened to Bear?"

She lowered her eyes, sadness passing briefly over her face. "He passed about ten years ago. He was always sitting right here on the porch, staring at the road, waiting for you."

Jimmy nodded, throat tightening. "At least he didn't forget me."

She searched his face, tears spilling quietly onto her cheeks. "You never opened my letters, did you?"

He felt heat rising in his face. "No. I didn't."

Her voice softened. "Then you don't know I left your dad years ago." She paused, stepping cautiously closer. "Jimmy, I wanted to see you. I wanted you to come home."

He took a sharp breath, unsteady, emotion flooding him in confusing waves—pain, resentment, regret, and beneath it all, something tender and long-forgotten now threatening to surface: love for his mother.

▪   ▪   ▪

In the sparse conference room, Sara faced five serious administrators gathered around the polished table: the Academic Director, Clinical Director, Case Manager, Oversight Committee Representative, and the facility Superintendent. A small window showed the sky outside through bars. The clock on the wall ticked loudly.

"We're here to vote on the continuation of Behavioral Wealthology," the Superintendent began neutrally. "Sara, your evaluation is on file, but we have a few questions."

Sara folded her hands, composed, bracing for the familiar skepticism toward unconventional curriculum ideas.

The Oversight Representative cleared his throat. "The $100,000 savings goal—realistically, isn't that setting these boys up to fail?"

"It's ambitious by design," Sara said carefully. "The goal challenges their assumptions about what's possible. The instructor showed them exactly how it can be done through small daily actions. It is realistic—and he taught the boys to expect it."

The Clinical Director frowned slightly. "About that—your report mentions this 'Expectancy Experiment.' Isn't that based on the idea of manifesting or calling upon some spiritual assistance? Isn't that problematic?"

Sara hesitated briefly, knowing the reaction she risked. But she wouldn't back away—not now.

"It is about expectancy," she said clearly, gently. "And yes, it's spiritual. It suggests that believing in a goal can invite unseen assistance—call it coincidence, synchronicity, or whatever you're comfortable with. But it works, and I saw it happen with these boys. At the very least, it cultivates faith in their goals."

The Superintendent exhaled slowly, shaking his head. "Sara, you've always been the pragmatic voice here. Can you honestly stand behind something like this?"

Sara met his eyes calmly, steadily. "Yes," she replied quietly. "I can, and I am."

She allowed the silence to linger, feeling—for once—unburdened by their skepticism. Who were they to judge her anyway?

．　．　．

They stood facing each other awkwardly on the porch, both

unsure what to do next.

"Let's sit on the swing," his mother said softly. "Like we used to in the evenings, remember?"

She looked old, he thought, older than her age.

Jimmy walked silently to the swing and felt the familiar creak as he sat down. She joined him, saying nothing. For a moment, only silence filled the space between them.

"You're angry," she said. "You have the right to be."

He drew a slow breath, finding his voice. "I just don't understand how you could do it. I was sixteen years old. I was terrified, alone, vulnerable, and imprisoned because of what I'd done. Do you have any idea how much guilt I carried? And then—when I needed you most—you abandoned me."

He stared at the cracked porch boards, unable to look up, his voice barely above a whisper. "How could you do that to me?"

She sat still, tears rolling silently down her face. Finally, she spoke quietly, her voice trembling. "I don't know."

He turned toward her bitterly. "You don't know? That's your answer after all these years? You just don't know?"

"I was weak, Jimmy. I let your father control me completely. It's no excuse. It's just the truth. I should've protected you, stood by you... but I let fear in my own marriage keep me silent."

He glared at her, seeing the deep lines of sorrow etched on her face, feeling his own throat tighten.

"You were my mother. You were supposed to fight for me," he said softly.

Her voice broke. "I've lived with that failure every day since. It's my life's greatest regret. I can't forgive myself. The only real question now," she said, looking into his eyes, "is can you?"

. . .

"There's a lot more to this course than the Expectancy Experiment," Sara said evenly, "which, in fact, is an optional daily routine. The heart of Behavioral Wealthology is structured daily action, consistent habits, and clear accountability."

The smug Oversight Committee Rep raised an eyebrow skeptically. "Accountability—among a group of social outcasts who are notoriously resistant to structure?"

Sara leaned forward slightly, keeping her voice calm. "Exactly. The daily structure gives them something concrete, manageable. And the accountability makes them realize, maybe for the first time, they could control their futures."

The Clinical Director folded his arms. "But Sara, you understand our concern. Aren't we risking false hope? Especially given their histories—setting these kids up for disappointment?"

She took a measured breath, glancing briefly at each administrator before answering. "False hope implies there's no real possibility. But this course taught them to transform vague goals into daily habits. That's the whole point: it isn't false hope. It's about objective performance and quantifiable actions."

The Academic Director tapped his pen impatiently. "Yet your report emphasizes this '*Power Within*' which you opposed just two months ago. How exactly do you quantify that?"

"You don't," Sara said steadily "You witness it and score it. Every daily habit, every small effort, has been assigned specific point values in the 5-year crusade system. The boys track their own actions each day—earning points for productive habits, extra work hours, even resisting negative behaviors. It's objective, measurable, and extremely practical."

The Clinical Director leaned forward slightly, surprised. "A point system to score daily habits and behaviors?"

"Yes," Sara said, meeting his gaze squarely. "This system

takes their intangible progress and makes it concrete, visible, and trackable. Scoring is the heart of the entire course—and it's precisely how we measure success or failure."

The Superintendent studied her, his skepticism fading slightly. "Show us," he said finally, nodding toward the manual. "Explain exactly how these points work."

"Not only can I show you," she said, "I can give you my personal testimony after following the system for a month."

. . .

Jimmy sat motionless, her question lingering painfully between them. *Will I forgive you?* He felt the old, familiar ache rising—raw and exposed, as if it had been waiting all these years for exactly this moment. *How can I forgive you? You abandoned me. You left me alone, afraid, ashamed. How does anyone forgive that?*

He stared at his mother's weary eyes, suddenly recognizing how fragile she looked—smaller than he remembered, older, bearing scars he hadn't noticed before.

"I don't know," he finally said, his voice low. "I honestly don't know if I can. But I'll try. I promise—I'll try."

She nodded quietly, accepting the uncertainty in his words. After a long pause, she stood carefully.

"Wait here," she murmured, moving toward the door. "I have something for you."

When she returned, she handed him a worn envelope, its corners softened by time. It was marked in faded red letters: *Return to Sender.*

"This was the first letter I had the courage to write to you, years ago. It's not much, Jimmy—just what I needed you to hear back then. When the time is right, read it. Not now, of course."

He took it silently, his thumb tracing the faded handwriting.

She hesitated. "Will I ever see you again?"

Jimmy stood slowly, carefully slipping the letter into his jacket pocket. He looked at her gently, feeling the weight of all they'd left unsaid.

"I don't know, Mom," he answered honestly. "I just don't know."

Then he turned and walked slowly back to his car, the unanswered question drifting behind him. All he knew for sure was that he'd followed the pull of his soul, listened to the silent voice of the *Power Within,* and now experienced the peace that felt like freedom.

■ ■ ■

The Clinical Director eyed her, appearing genuinely interested for the first time during the meeting. "And you tested this system yourself?"

"Yes," Sara replied. "I followed it for a month, and it was eye-opening to see how little I was doing in my free time. The performance scoring doesn't lie—it significantly increased my self-awareness through tracking."

Sara opened the course manual, aware that every skeptical eye in the room was fixed squarely on her. She calmly flipped to a marked page, turned it toward the Superintendent, and steadied herself.

"Each habit or daily action is assigned a point value," she explained carefully. "Exercise, meditation, prioritizing top tasks, resisting negative habits—even dedicating extra hours toward personal goals—all of these earn points."

She hesitated briefly, feeling the familiar tug of vulnerability but pushing past it. Who were these old guys anyway? Why did she need their validation? Sara felt her inner power rising.

"Honestly, I started out skeptical—even dismissive. But when I tracked my own habits and daily points, something unexpected happened: I saw exactly how stuck I'd become. I also became aware of how conceited, arrogant, and wrong I was to dismiss this course, especially when I was part of a system that was failing these boys."

A collective tension filled the room.

"What I noticed almost immediately," she continued, "was how little effort I was giving compared to when I pursued my college and master's degrees. The scoring made it visible."

"Made what visible?" asked the Superintendent.

"My drifting. After my last master's degree, I simply stopped progressing. I showed up for my job, took care of my daughter, and convinced myself it was enough. But this scoring system revealed how little I'd actually challenged myself."

The smug Oversight Committee Representative frowned. "And what exactly have you done with this profound insight?"

Sara straightened, a new clarity and determination firming her expression. "I've started learning about nonprofits," she said assertively. "This course made me question what happens after kids leave juvenile detention. Maybe the real support they need is out there—in the community, beyond these walls. Since nothing ever changes here, maybe that's where I should be focusing next in my career."

Her words almost echoed in the silence. A fierce tension thickened in the room, in stark contrast to Sara's inner calm.

■　■　■

Jimmy pulled into the parking lot of the Wealthy Gardens winery and walked to a secluded spot at the property's edge—a small pond with two tombstones resting quietly on a knoll. Over the past ten years, since his mentor's passing, this had become hallowed ground, his private sanctuary, a place of tranquility.

He drew the envelope from his pocket, his thoughts heavy with memories of his aging mother. How could he simply forgive her now, when he was a grown man who no longer needed her? She was the one who needed him now, and perhaps it was her turn to feel what it was like to be abandoned and alone.

He opened the envelope carefully and began to read.

Jimmy,

I don't know if this letter will reach you. I don't know if you'll want to read it, and I understand if you don't. But I need you to know—I left him. I finally left your father.

I should have done it long ago. I should have stood up for you, defended you, visited you. I should have written sooner. There are so many regrets, I don't even know where to begin.

This letter isn't much. I'm not asking for anything. I just want you to know that you are not forgotten. Not by me.

I still think about you every day. I still love you. That never changed. I will always love and miss you until my last breath.

—Mom

Jimmy folded the letter carefully and looked out over the quiet pond. He felt something release deep within—not perfect forgiveness, perhaps, but a gentler acceptance. For the first time, he felt truly free as his vision became blurred with tears.

．　．　．

The Superintendent exhaled, studying her carefully. "Why do you believe so strongly in this, Sara?"

Sara sensed the familiar disrespect over her ideas—as if she were now naive for believing in a system based on simple, basic tasks. Sara knew the older man didn't truly care what she said; he was merely asking a perfunctory question.

"Because in 10 weeks, we saw 30 percent growth in attendance, 95 percent homework completion, and zero behavioral incidents. And it wasn't because someone forced them. They showed up because they wanted to. They asked for extra materials. They tracked their own habits. They began to believe in themselves. That's why I believe in this course of instruction."

The Academic Director frowned. "It still relies on that 'Power Within' concept. Are you saying you're comfortable now with basing rehabilitation on something so...ambiguous?"

Sara nodded firmly. "It's not doctrine. It's not mystical. It's disciplined belief in one's own potential. And yes, I was once a cynic. I thought it was vague, soft, even dangerous." She looked around the room, no longer apologetic. "But I was wrong. The real danger is pretending our current methods are working when they're not. We're failing the boys—and we know it."

A long silence followed.

The Superintendent folded his hands. "We've heard your case, loud and clear. Final recommendation?"

Sara spoke with authority. "The course should continue—unchanged. It should be offered during prime hours, not tucked away at night like an afterthought. Students should have access to listening devices for affirmations. I've sourced the equipment, and the instructor will cover the cost. And students who volunteer for work duties because of the course should be eligible for parole consideration. I've written and filed all the necessary paperwork. I'll handle all follow-up—unpaid, if needed."

She closed the manual softly and waited.

The Superintendent nodded. "Let's vote."

Minutes later, the course was approved—barely—as a night elective. All four of Sara's additional recommendations were rejected. The room emptied quickly. Sara remained in her chair, hands resting on the closed manual, her chest hollow yet oddly calm. The vote confirmed what she had known for some time: her voice had never really been heard here.

That afternoon, she received an email: she would no longer oversee the course and would return to normal admin duties.

The following day, Sara turned in her resignation. Walking to her car afterward, she felt a calm reassurance despite the uncertainty of the future. It was the *Power Within,* an intangible instinct that spoke without words. And it felt like freedom.

CHAPTER 14

5 Years Later

The Students

Five years later, the students defied every likely statistic. Only 6% returned to incarceration, dramatically outperforming the national recidivism rate of 67%. Among the successful majority, 40% had saved at least $10,000, another 20% had built savings exceeding $50,000, and an impressive 10% reached or surpassed the ambitious goal of $100,000. Even the remaining 30%, who lived paycheck-to-paycheck without savings, maintained their freedom—along with optimism for future possibilities.

The Course

Behavioral Wealthology expanded rapidly beyond the classroom, spreading nationwide to juvenile detention centers, adult prisons, schools, and community programs. While critics derided its structured rigor and central concept of a *Power Within*, continuous success stories flooded social media, inspiring countless others to adopt the tracking system. In time, testimonials of transformed lives went viral, fueling a movement built on timeless habits, relentless discipline, and undeniable results.

Slugs

Slugs left the reformatory determined to open his own auto repair shop. Initially, he struggled to maintain consistent habits and soon stopped tracking crusade points altogether. After enrolling in trade school, he gave it an earnest effort but ultimately struggled with the certification exams, deciding entrepreneurship wasn't his path after all. Instead, Slugs found steady work as a dealership mechanic. Five years later, he hasn't achieved wealth or ownership, but he's debt-free, content with a simpler life and a realistic aspiration to become the service manager.

Mack

Mack's arrogance became his downfall. Initially chasing a million-dollar dream without discipline, he bounced between low-paying jobs, alienating supervisors with his stubborn defiance and disrespectful attitude. Repeated firings led him back to the streets, where his natural bravado and strength found darker purposes. Mack became an enforcer for a local gambling ring, quickly gaining a dangerous reputation. But power bred recklessness, and after a violent confrontation over unpaid debts, Mack was arrested, convicted, and sentenced for voluntary manslaughter. Five years later, he sits behind bars, the tragic architect of his own destruction, his bravado replaced by bitter silence.

Jamal

After release, Jamal started working full-time as a nursing assistant to pay bills and support himself. He tracked every habit, hour, and extra effort taught in the course, staying disciplined with his daily routines. With steady paychecks and careful budgeting, Jamal saved enough money to cover what his scholarships and grants didn't. He first enrolled in community college, later transferring to a state university, always balancing classes with a part-time campus job. By consistently sticking to the system—logging job hours, study hours, and habits on the app—he built a reliable structure for his life. Now, five years later, Jamal has earned strong letters of recommendation and is preparing to take the Medical College Admission Test (MCAT), steadily moving toward his goal of becoming a doctor.

Sara

While searching for a more fulfilling job in social work, Sara worked part-time in a temporary role with Jimmy to scale the course. Within a year, through tireless effort and successful grant applications, Sara transformed Behavioral Wealthology from a classroom elective into a fully established nonprofit organization. She became its full-time director, rapidly scaling its impact nationwide by certifying teachers, developing digital curricula, and implementing the system across juvenile centers, adult prisons, and schools. As Behavioral Wealthology grew, Sara emerged as a nationally respected figure in prison reform, achieving financial stability and modeling strength and integrity for her daughter, Faith. During this exciting period of growth, Sara married a man who shared her vision for social work.

Jimmy

Jimmy remained exactly where his heart had always led him—in the classroom, teaching Behavioral Wealthology directly, quietly transforming lives one student at a time. Earning his PhD amplified his credibility, but he deliberately chose simplicity and meaningful connection over proving himself through achievement. Jimmy continued mentoring, teaching online certification classes, and guiding students toward brighter futures, realizing the happiness he'd always sought came from genuine human connection—the missing piece in his lifestyle puzzle. And in the quiet contentment of his home, with Sara by his side and Faith filling their days with joy, Jimmy finally understood that the richest life wasn't something he built; it was something he received. And it was more than he had ever imagined.

THE END

CHAPTER 15

Now What?

As the author of this story, I now reflect on its conclusion. It has been seven long years since my first book, *The Wealthy Gardener*, was published, and those who know me well will say I spend a great deal of time alone in my home office. I often think about this solitude and why finishing this book was so important to me. Reflecting on this, I'm reminded of the most influential book of my youth, *Think and Grow Rich*, which I read four decades ago and which fundamentally altered my perspective. Great books have the power to change lives.

I wonder now: will *5-Year Crusade* possess the elusive magic of influential books, or will it become just another volume gathering dust on a shelf? Will it genuinely alter your daily actions in a tangible way?

Having read this book, you now understand the 5-year crusade system to free the *Power Within* — but what next?

When you finish a book filled with actionable advice, it's crucial to be aware of the forgetting curve. Research suggests that people forget 80–90% of the information they read within a month unless they actively reinforce or apply what they've learned. To prevent this primary cause of failure, immediate active engagement is essential.

Without engagement, nothing else matters.

You've traveled alongside Jimmy, Sara, and Jamal, witnessing how disciplined action can rewrite destinies. Now it's your turn. Let's discuss how to apply this book, utilize its system, and prepare to implement actions and habits capable of changing your life. Here are some helpful tools to get you started.

Tool #1: The Crusader's Tracker app

The Crusader's Tracker app is designed to help you track hours and habits as outlined in this system. In fact, *this app is the system.* You can download it for free from the Apple App Store or Google Play Store. For detailed instructions, visit 5yearcrusade.com.

Tool #2: Guided Meditations

The Crusader's Creed and Expectancy guided meditations are designed to be customized by you to reflect your specific goals, obstacles, and current situation. To get started quickly, listen to the pre-recorded meditations on the **Audios** page of the Crusader's Tracker app or download the recordings as MP3 files at 5yearcrusade.com. Both options provide a solid starting point, but it's even more effective to customize your own Crusader's Creed and Expectancy guided meditations. You can download the meditation scripts from 5yearcrusade.com and make them your own. Listening regularly to these recordings significantly increases your likelihood of initiating, maintaining, and sustaining the actions and habits essential to your 5-year crusade.

Tool #3: Weekly Planner

If you want a weekly planner tailored specifically to your 5-year crusade, try *The Crusader's Planner: A Weekly System for High Achievers*, which closely follows the blueprint in this book. It helps you identify your most important weekly tasks and track precisely how you use your 5 to 20 impact hours each week. *The Crusader's Planner* also includes daily affirmations and monthly inspirational passages aligned with the core principles of your 5-year crusade.

Tool #4: Crusade Calculator

Customize your 5-year crusade but stay accountable. To calculate your weekly point goal for your 5-year crusade, open the Crusader's Tracker app and navigate to the Settings page. Enter your chosen settings for job hours, impact hours, daily habits, and vices for your habit fast. Based on these inputs, the calculator will generate your recommended weekly point range. In addition to determining your weekly goal, the Crusader's Tracker app will help you consistently track your progress.

Tool #5: Physical Scorecards

Tracking is challenging without a real-time checklist. While memory-based tracking at day's end is possible, using a physical index card with a checklist is far more effective in a daily system. You can download these index scorecards at 5yearcrusade.com. You'll find a PDF template for printing onto a single sheet of paper. After printing, cut along the dotted lines to create six index cards that serve as physical checklists. If you're printing or making custom index cards, aim for 110 lb. to 140 lb. cardstock, which is standard for index cards. I used this exact scorecard on heavy stock while writing this book (before developing the Crusader's Tracker app).

Tool #6: Exercise shoes and Venue

You need athletic shoes and a suitable place for daily exercise. Simple, effective workouts are best. Group gym sessions can be motivating, but quick home workouts might fit your schedule better. Adapt your exercise plans based on the weather. In Pittsburgh, I maintain a flexible plan to accommodate cold winters and rainy days. I prefer running or biking outdoors, but often switch to indoor options such as a treadmill, stationary bike, or a gym with a pool. Flexibility is essential for maintaining consistency in an exercise program.

Tool #7: Smart Phone

To change your reality, track how much time you spend in "non-reality." Check your phone's digital wellbeing or screen time feature to identify how much time you spend on social media, podcasts, news outlets, and similar activities. Consider setting app-usage limits or going cold turkey with a 30-day habit fast to break away from poor habits. During my most productive years, I eliminated all passive activities, such as watching sports, television, social media, and movies. Instead, I engaged in meaningful pursuits and ultimately had more fun.

Tool #8: Meditation App

A daily meditation practice of 5, 10, or 15 minutes is one of the most important habits you can adopt to increase your happiness set point, inner peace, and emotional regulation. Over time, meditation strengthens your brain—specifically, the prefrontal cortex, which is responsible for executive functions, impulse control, and the ability to choose delayed gratification. Daily meditation, whether silent or guided, offers numerous benefits. Find a quality meditation app, download it, and practice consistently.

Tool #9: Desk Timer

Tracking impact hours often involves logging time spent at a desk. An inexpensive desk timer with a count-up or countdown feature can be helpful. A desk timer is a device used for managing time to complete important tasks. It can also help you tackle less desirable tasks by setting a fixed duration, such as one hour, to focus on them. As I type these words, a desk timer sits visibly in front of my keyboard. When I stand, I pause the timer. The Crusader's Tracker app also includes a timer specifically for this purpose.

Tool #10: *Daily Crusade: A Year of Meditations for High Achievers*

My most cherished tool of all is this daily meditation book designed to support ambitious goal achievers on their crusade. Being a crusader can feel lonely at times because the world is constantly pulling you away from your purpose. Many people won't understand your ambition or why you choose to sacrifice for your dreams, leaving you to sustain your spirit independently each day. *The Daily Crusade* is written as a message from the *Power Within,* urging you to stay the course throughout your 5-year crusade. It emphasizes small efforts, daily habits, and an attitude of expectancy to maintain consistent progress.

In parting, I'll admit my goal for this book was audacious: I envisioned future success stories and reader testimonials. Driven by this expectation, I felt compelled to create a supportive ecosystem to help readers of *5-Year Crusade.* Now, I consider *The Crusader's Planner* and *The Daily Crusade* even more essential than the original *5-Year Crusade* book, as these supportive companions will stay with you throughout your journey toward your ambitious goals. Please consider exploring this ecosystem of support at **5yearcrusade.com.** These resources are designed to be purchased once and utilized now and indefinitely—alongside the all-in-one master tool, the Crusader's Tracker app.

Crusade Resources

The Crusader's Tracker app

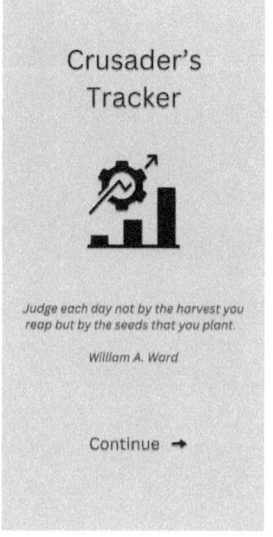

Customizable settings (choose your own habits) • Track daily habits • Track daily hours • Keep daily and weekly scores • Timer • Recordings of Crusader's Creed affirmation and Expectancy Guided Meditation • Voice Recorder • The Premium version includes rotating affirmations (with selectable themes such as expectation, discipline, sacrifice, optimism, etc.). You can also unlock access to a full history of past weekly scores, revealing trends over time for better or worse.

5yearcrusade.com

- Step by step instructions for getting started on your own 5-year crusade now.
- Useful links to recommended resources.
- Audios of the Crusader's Creed affirmations and the Expectancy Guided Meditation.
- Crusader's Tracker app instructions.
- Download printable physical scorecards.
- Downloadable scripts to make your own personal recordings.

The next 2 pages are a look inside the book.

JN/JUL

Most important things to do this week

_____
_____
_____
_____
_____

---

30 Mon   I win today, and that is enough

Habits _____
Hours _____
Total _____

---

1 Tues   I follow what ignites and energizes me

Habits _____
Hours _____
Total _____

---

2 Wed   Through extra effort I refine talents into skills

Habits _____
Hours _____
Total _____

---

3 Thu   I set bold goals and pursue them with faith

Habits _____
Hours _____
Total _____

JUL

What I did for impact this week

_____

_____

_____

_____

_____

I spend myself in a cause that matters **Fri 4**

_____
Habits

_____
Hours

_____
Total

I free myself from nonbeneficial behaviors **Sat 5**

_____
Habits

_____
Hours

_____
Total

I respect my need to unplug and restore **Sun 6**

_____
Habits

_____
Hours

_____
Total

Luck, Coincidence, Ideas

THIS WEEK

Habits _____

Hours _____

TOTAL _____

The next 2 pages are a look inside the book.

NOTE the daily <u>affirmations</u> in the *Crusader's Planner* match the daily <u>meditations</u> in *Daily Crusade*

July 4

Daily Meditation: The Sacred Effort

It is by spending oneself that one becomes rich.
– Sarah Bernhardt

Listen to me, you will not find fulfillment in holding back, in conserving your strength for some distant day. The deepest satisfaction is reserved for those who pour themselves fully into a worthy cause, who leave nothing undone that could have been done.

You were not made to coast through life, half-engaged, half-invested, and half-interested. You were made to give yourself fully—to your work, to your purpose, to your vision. Do not fear exhaustion; fear only the regret of never having given your all. There is no greater fulfillment than knowing you have done your best, that you have held nothing in reserve when it mattered most.

Many wander through life, never knowing the deep peace that comes from a sacred effort. They do enough to get by, but never enough to be transformed. You are called to more. The fullness of your potential is unlocked only when you commit fully, when you refuse to settle, when you give the best of yourself even when no one is watching.

At the end of this day, let there be no doubt: You gave all that could be given. And in that, you will find a richness that no comfort or convenience can ever provide.

Affirmation: I give my best today. I spend myself fully in a cause that matters. I hold nothing back so at the end of this day, I will know the exhaustion and the deepest satisfaction of a well-lived day.

July 5

Daily Meditation: Reset Your Mind

Your vices are just habits that feel good but harm you.
Unlearn your vices with a habit fast. — 5-Year Crusade

You were not created to be ruled by impulses. I did not place you in this life to chase distractions, to numb your spirit with noise, or to settle for pleasures that leave you empty. You were made for more—for focus, for depth, for a life rich with meaning and power.

Yet the world pulls at you. It bombards you with stimulation, tempts you with quick rewards, and scatters your thoughts until you forget who you are. But I have not forgotten. I am calling you now—back to yourself.

It is time to reset. Step away from the habits that steal your clarity. Strip away what is shallow and see what remains. For thirty days, free yourself from the flood of cheap dopamine. Without it, your mind will sharpen. Your energy will return. Your joy will deepen.

This is not punishment. This is power. It is the proof that you are not ruled by your cravings—you are led by your calling. Each day you resist what weakens you, your true self rises. The self that lives with discipline. The self that leads. The self that remembers.

You are not here to be distracted. You are here to build. Begin now.

Affirmation: I free myself from impulses and self-sabotage. I choose clarity over chaos, discipline overindulgence, and depth over emptiness. My mind is sharp. I reclaim the fullness of my power.

The *5-Year Crusade* is the sequel to *The Wealthy Gardener*, a book written as a father's financial advice to his son. Its short chapters and hybrid format—blending fiction and nonfiction—make it an accessible read despite its length. Currently, more than 87 percent of reviewers give it a five-star rating on Amazon, and the audiobook holds a #1-rated badge in its category. As a resource for understanding the underlying system of a 5-year crusade, this book is essential for your library.

The Wealthy Bookheads

Receive educational 2-minute book bites for life-long learning. We research life-changing books and curate their golden wisdom. Why not visit wealthbookheads.com to check out our small but growing library of book reviews staged in a question-and-answer format to increase your engagement? Grow smarter every week in the next five years.

Self-Shackles Questionnaire

(A "Yes" answer indicates the
presence of an inner shackle)

Self-Delusion

1. Do you have big goals or dreams but rarely work 5 to 20 overtime hours every week to earn them?

2. Do you believe you're "on the right path" even though you lack clear goals for this week, month, and year?

3. Do you tell sometimes tell yourself that you'll do the hard task tomorrow, even when you have time to do it today?

4. Do you believe you can achieve more than average results without working more than average people?

5. Do you have a big goal without a tracking system to log how much time you're giving to achieve it each week?

Self-Neglect

1. Do you sometimes skip your full workout on a busy day, even when you could fit in a shorter workout?

2. Do you regularly feel too busy, drained, or emotionally exhausted to exercise for just 15 minutes every day?

3. Do you ever feel like your responsibilities are so important that you don't have time to indulge in exercise?

4. Do you ever feel anxious, worried, or irritable without regularly exercising to shift your mental state?

5. Do you wait to feel motivated before taking care of your health, rather than building a nonnegotiable routine?

Self-Sabotage

1. Do you procrastinate or surrender to impulses even when they conflict with your highest goals or best self?
2. Do you often engage in habits or activities that feel good in the moment but waste your time and potential?
3. When you feel stressed out, do you often turn to escape activities, distractions, or a drink to "take the edge off" rather than confronting the source of your stress?
4. Do you find yourself choosing tension-relieving activities over goal-achieving activities in your free time?
5. Do you avoid tracking bad habits like screen time because deep down you don't want to face the truth?

Self-Doubt

1. Do you often feel overwhelmed by how far you have to go, rather than focusing on the step you can do today?
2. Do you sometimes experience fear, doubt, and worry in your free time when you think about your challenges?
3. Do you set big goals that look glamorous but avoid scheduling mundane weekly hours to earn them?
4. Do you frequently compare yourself to others, feeling envious as if they have it all together but you don't?
5. Do you often feel imprisoned and stuck due to your lack of money, support, opportunity, or free time?

Self-Contempt

1. Have you ever downplayed your dreams, defending your view reasonable, practical, and realistic?
2. Do you struggle to expect the best outcome for your life goals, knowing without a doubt that you are worthy?

3. Do you criticize yourself more harshly for mistakes than you would criticize a friend for the same thing?

4. When you fall short of a goal or give in to a bad habit, do you question what's wrong with you as a person?

5. Have you stopped believing in miracles for your life, and started resigning yourself to average conditions?

The Crusader's Creed

Structured to confront and overcome five common self-imposed barriers—Self-Delusion, Self-Neglect, Self-Sabotage, Self-Doubt, and Self-Contempt—this creed serves as a powerful reminder to stay aligned with your highest ambitions. Listen daily to refocus your energy, affirm your worth, strengthen your resilience, and commit to the purposeful habits that transform ambitious goals into reality. It's not perfect. If it seems overwhelming at first, stay with it. With repeated listening, there will come a day when it no longer feels overwhelming or like "too much." Listen to it on the Crusader's Tracker app.

Introduction

God grant me the serenity today, accept the things I cannot change, the courage to change the things I can, and the wisdom to know the difference. Today is an important day of my life. I have been given this day to use as I will. I can waste it or use it for good. What I do today is important because I am exchanging a day of my life for it. When tomorrow comes, this day will be gone forever; in its place is something that I have left behind; let it be something good. I focus now on these mindset affirmations to avoid forgetting what matters most in this one day.

Self-Delusion

Recognizing that it's impossible to achieve [insert your goal or goals] with vague desires, unclear plans, and a common life-style, I defeat the shackle of self-delusion by choosing the easy way of reminding myself that I want [insert your goal or goals] more than anything. I want it because [insert your deepest motives], and I vow to pay the price of 5 to 20 hours every week for as long as it takes to earn it. To get more than average results, I work more than average people this week. I am defined by what I do, not by what I say I will do. Therefore, I focus on building good habits, taking consistent daily actions, and tracking both my habits and hours to avoid self-deceit. I sacrifice many ordinary things in my free time to do the vital few things that lead to an extraordinary life. I am the kind of person who turns goals into reality through 5 to 20 extra weekly hours. To prevent the shackle of self-delusion, I know exactly what I want most, I focus on why I want it, and then I track my habits and hours to focus on the process of earning it.

Self-Neglect

Recognizing that it's impossible to achieve [insert your goal or goals] when I feel tired, overwhelmed, or emotionally off-balance, I defeat the shackle of self-neglect by choosing the easy way of daily physical exertion. I am the kind of person who prioritizes health and fitness to strengthen my emotional resilience, mental clarity, and inner drive. I let no day pass without movement be-cause I know that mood follows motion. When I feel down, I move. When I feel resistance to move, I focus on the first step—the act of starting. On busy days, I choose a short workout over none at all, knowing that exercise consistency matters more than exercise intensity. To avoid the shackle of self-neglect, I move daily to activate my best state of mind.

Self-Sabotage

Recognizing that it's impossible to achieve [insert your goal or goals] while I'm held back by nonbeneficial habits and vices, I defeat the shackle of self-sabotage by choosing the crusade way of eliminating temptations that don't align with my goal of [insert your goal or goals]. I am the kind of person who lives freely, without the weight of self-sabotaging behaviors, vices, or socially accepted addictions. I reject any-thing that feels good in the moment but harms me in the long run. To break the grip of unwanted habits that are not aligned with my highest purpose, I commit to a habit fast plus a daily meditation to re-condition my brain for peak performance.

Self-Doubt

Recognizing that it's impossible to achieve [insert your goal or goals] when I don't believe in myself, I defeat the shackle of self-doubt by choosing the easy way of focusing on small, con-sistent efforts—one day at a time. I understand that the path to [insert your goal or goals] is paved by winning today, and then tomorrow, and then the next day, so I commit to living in day-tight compartments. I trust that I was given ambition for a rea-son, and that no obstacle can withstand a steady river of daily impactful hours. I measure a good day by what I do, not by how I feel. I know that self-engagement is the cure for self-doubt, and productive work is the cure for unproductive worry. To eliminate the shackle of self-doubt, I plan my work,

work my plan, get into motion, and stay in motion—always focused on the most important thing I can do today.

Self-Contempt

Recognizing that it's impossible to achieve [insert your goal or goals] when I don't believe I'm worthy of them, I defeat the shackle of self-contempt by choosing the easy way of honest self-appreciation. I acknowledge that I possess the key qualities of resilience, discipline, and optimism—and I have demonstrated these qualities in my past. I understand that I am vulnerable to forgetting my strengths when I fall short of my goals, when I give in to old habits, when I feel discouraged by slow progress, or when I face criticism from others. In those moments, I vow to be my own best friend, even as I hold myself to high standards. To eliminate the shackle of self-contempt, I meditate on [insert your goal or goals] with calm expectation, reflect on my best qualities, and never question my self-worth. In fact, am so worthy that even the Universe is for me, assisting me in response to my expectations.

In summary, my life today is a crusade, a vigorous movement for a worthy cause. As I perform the habits of self-empowerment, and the actions of self-engagement, I am getting better and better, every day in every way. I am the *Power Within.*

Acknowledgements

I want to acknowledge those who contributed directly to bringing this book to life. My deepest thanks to Mike Soforic, my developmental editor, who worked through the rawest chapter drafts and helped shape the book; my vigilant copy editors who cleaned up versions of this book that I eventually decided to trash; Dennis Kleinman, narrator of the audiobook who made the story come alive; a few beta readers who gave me feedback; Eldar Sufiyanov, developer of the Crusader's Tracker app; and mostly, to my wife, Patti, whose support, patience, and wisdom carried me to the finish line. Thank you all for patiently standing by me during the process of creation.

Start Here

5yearcrusade.com